THE SEARCH
FOR LEADERSHIP

There Can Be No Dedication
Without Education

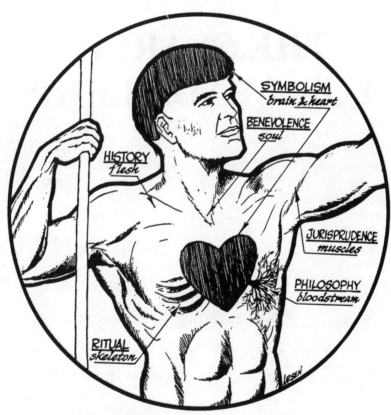

The Body of Freemasonry

Allen E. Roberts

The Search for Leadership

Leadership
Principles
Planning
Communications
Building
Control
Guides
Points
Cartoons
Potpourri
Tips

A Publication of Research Lodge No. 2,
Ancient, Free and Accepted Masons, Iowa

Distributed by Macoy Publishing & Masonic Supply Co., Inc.

Anchor Communications
Highland Springs, Virginia

DEDICATED to those Lodges of Research that are attempting to carry Free-masonry into the 21st century as a viable force for the benefit of mankind, and to those Freemasons who share their lives, resources, knowledge, ideas, and love with their fellowman regardless of his color, creed, politics, or religious faith.

BOOKS BY ALLEN E. ROBERTS

House Undivided: The Story of Freemasonry and the Civil War
Freemasonry in Highland Springs
Sword and Trowel
Masonry Under Two Flags
Key To Freemasonry's Growth
How To Conduct a Successful Leadership Seminar
Freemasonry's Servant
Fifty Golden Years
Brotherhood in Action
The Craft and Its Symbols
G. Washington: Master Mason
Frontier Cornerstone
Shedding Light on Leadership
A Chronicle of Virginia Research Lodge
Freemasonry in American History
Who Is Who In Freemasonry
Brother Truman
La Francmasoneria Y Sus Simbolos
The Diamond Years

MOTION PICTURES WRITTEN, PRODUCED AND DIRECTED

The Pilot
Growing the Leader
Breaking Barriers to Communication
Planning Unlocks the Door
People Make the Difference

The Brotherhood of Man . . .
Challenge!
Precious Heritage
Lonely World
"Fraternally Yours"
Virtue Will Triumph
Living Stones . . .

The Saga of the Holy Royal Arch of Freemasonry

Foreword

In his revised *Facts for Freemasons,* the late Harold Van Buren Voorhis, FPS, Life, and a Past President of The Philalethes Society, was asked: "What Masonic author and educator has probably done more than any other in modern times to further and encourage Masonic education?"

Voorhis answered: "Allen E. Roberts, author of several books including the very popular *The Craft and Its Symbols,* written especially for the newly raised Master Mason to answer questions raised in his mind after taking the degrees. Producer of the Masonic Educational Training Program films (5); *The Brotherhood of Man...* documentary for the M.S.A. His books, *House Undivided* and *Key To Freemasonry's Growth* have both gone into several printings."

Coming from one of America's most knowledgeable Freemasons and authors, that is high praise, indeed. But for those who do not know Allen (or, Al, as most of us who do know him well call him), this may need expanding.

In the Foreword I wrote for his *Freemasonry in American History* I said (among other things): "In my opinion, Allen Roberts is the most knowledgeable Masonic educator of the present day. He has taken contemporary management techniques and has applied them to Freemasonry. Naturally, he isn't universally popular. Men of little minds and big egos take strong exception when someone shows them what they have been doing wrong. The one strident voice, crying in the wilderness (or, perhaps whimpering in the back pasture), making itself heard over the sounds of the general acclaim, is ignored as much as possible.

"Al Roberts has taken his lumps. The honors so justly his due have never been paid him."

As a professional editor, not a Masonic editor, but a professional, I am appalled at the amount of work which Allen puts in on each project and the small amount of profit he has ever made. If he were to apply the same amount of energy and time to some professional endeavor, he would become independently wealthy. Instead he works for the fraternity which he loves. He never knows until a film or other project ends whether he will lose money on it.

A case in point is the six part series on leadership he wrote for *The Phila-lethes* magazine. This, along with his regular column "Through Masonic Windows" realizes no coin of the realm for him. He knows he will receive no monetary reward for the hundreds of hours he devotes to these and other Masonic projects. Yet, he feels if he can convince just one Master Mason who reads what he writes that Freemasonry is worth working for, his payment will be complete.

In 1969 Al wrote *Key To Freemasonry's Growth,* the first (and only) attempt to put the principles of management to work for the Craft. This book is still as modern as today. If you are truly interested in Masonic education and leadership, get the book, read and study it, along with this one. You'll be glad you did!

Jerry Marsengill

Preface

In 1982 Iowa Research Lodge No. 2 published *Shedding Light on Leadership*. The book, a paper back, went into several printings. Because of its acceptance by the Craft, the Lodge wanted the book enlarged and printed in a more durable form. So, we have *The Search For Leadership*.

The search for a title wasn't easy. We wanted one that would be fully descriptive of its contents, so we couldn't get away from "Leadership." That's what this book is all about — the cry (with all its synonyms) for leadership in Freemasonry. And Freemasonry isn't alone in its need for this illusive ingredient. Far too many profit, non-profit and governmental instrumentalities are wailing in this wilderness.

This search began for me on April Fools' Day 1948, the day I became a Master Mason. That's when my quest started for Masonic knowledge, information, light, or call it what you will. This search hasn't been easy. At times it has been so frustrating I've thrown up my hands and quit — but only for a moment. This beautiful system called "Freemasonry" is too excellent to let human beings destroy it.

The more questions I asked in my early days in the Craft the more annoyed the leadership became with me. I was accused, among other more unpleasant things, of "rocking the boat." It was strongly suggested I stick to learning the ritual. So I did.

The ritual came easily to me because I loved it. Then it was strongly suggested I slow up or I'd never get anywhere in Freemasonry. Several Past Masters of my lodge believed I was pushing myself, so I had to give the lectures in other lodges. Although I was nominated for Junior Deacon (the first elective office in my lodge), I was never elected to the office. Eight years later I was elected Senior Deacon. In 1959, in spite of concerted opposition, I was elected Master.

It was in 1955 that I began to see some light at the end of what had been a tunnel of darkness. During a church service that my lodge had been invited to attend, a retired minister told a story about Joseph Fort Newton. The act of Masonic Brotherly Love he described that took place during the American Civil War amazed and thrilled me. It changed my life forever. It turned me into a Masonic researcher and writer, and consequently an attempt to become a Masonic educator.

The search for more truths about what Freemasons did during the Civil War brought me in touch with Carl H. Claudy of The Masonic Service Association. Through him I learned there was much information about Freemasonry in existence, and there was, and always will be, a need for more. Because of my close connections with the MSA I later acquired one of the best friends I'll ever have — Conrad Hahn.

In 1957 the Grand Lodge of Virginia revitalized a long dormant committee called "Masonic Information, Research and Publications." This was a long-winded attempt to disguise what too many Grand Lodges consider a nasty word — "education." I was invited to attend its first meeting as a representative of the "grass roots." Precedence was broken! I wasn't a Past Master! And a year later I was made a member of the committee.

During the same year I became a member of Virginia Research Lodge No. 1777 which had been chartered in 1951. In 1966 I became its Master; with the death of Archer B. Gay in 1973, the secretary. My search for Masonic information was expanding.

Which brings me to reason for this publication that Jerry Marsengill has been asking me to write. What I've related may explain why I was determined early in my Masonic life to do everything possible to pass along what I might discover in my quest. It's the reason I've written articles and books. It's the reason for the motion pictures for Freemasonry I've produced. It's the reason I didn't think this was enough.

For years I've wanted to see a national Masonic publication on the scope of the old *Life* magazine. I wanted to see one that was independent (by this I mean not a "house organ") that would adhere to the landmarks of the Craft (whatever they are). I suggested this to the MSA several years ago. I had seen copies of the excellent *The Master Mason* published by the MSA years ago. What I didn't know at the time was the MSA must walk a tight line; it's a voluntary organization; it can be demolished by the Grand Lodges; it's impossible for it to be "independent." This I learned when I wrote its history in 1967.

At the urging of several Masons I started *The Altar Light,* a newsletter for Master Masons. The first issue was mailed to a handful of subscribers in May 1977. Conrad Hahn, my friend of twenty years, said of it: "You have achieved your primary objectives; keeping the reader informed about what is happening in the Masonic world. You can't have too many of these informative pieces. Almost 20 such items in this issue. You've touched your other bases with editorials, a long biography, book reviews, good and wholesome instruction and illustrations. Variety is the spice of life."

Connie died shortly after he noted his inimitable comments on the fourth edition. Some of his notes will be included with some of the articles reproduced from *The Altar Light.*

Jerry and I, along with a few others who love Freemasonry, have long believed only excellent, knowledgeable, dedicated Masonic leadership is going to keep the organization viable. He asked me to keep the articles about leadership that appeared in *The Altar Light* alive by including them in this book. He also wanted them to reach a wider audience.

Articles are also included from other sources, particularly *The Philalethes*. This magazine has become what I had hoped we would one day have in Freemasonry — an international *independent* Masonic publication. In recent years it has abolished censorship in any form. It presents every side of every story, thereby accepting the truth that Freemasons are among the most intelligent of men. They have the right to all the facts so they can determine the course of action they should take. Naturally, this doesn't please everyone, but it has met with wide-spread acclaim.

For three years I published *The Altar Light*. During this period Macoy Publishing and Masonic Supply Co. wanted to take it over as a "house organ" with me as the editor. I finally agreed. Two years later someone at Macoy determined it was too expensive, and it was terminated. Jerry called, and with his tongue-in-his-cheek sympathized with me. In almost the same breath he asked me to continue writing the column originated in the *AL*, "Through Masonic Windows," for *The Philalethes*. I agreed.

There will be some repetition in this book. The articles and talks have been recorded over a long period of time. They have been spoken and written for widely differing audiences. You will find there are some subjects I highly favor. But I have tried to keep the repetition at a minimum. There are, however, some topics that should be covered over and over again.

As we continue our search for leadership, perhaps some of the points recorded in this book will strike a responsive chord. If something said here causes you to dig deeper into the fascinating subject of Freemasonry and leadership, our hopes will be fulfilled.

May you receive as much enjoyment from reading what follows as I have in passing it along.

Allen E. Roberts
Highland Springs,
Virginia July 4, 1987

Contents

Potpourri

Illustrations

Shedding Light on Leadership

From the beginning to the end of our Masonic careers the learning of the ritual is stressed. Thousands of dollars are spent to perpetuate the learning and retaining of the ritual. Little is set aside to teach Freemasons what the ritual means. That would be "Masonic education." The word "education" frightens far too many of us.

Grand Lodges, the few doing anything about spreading Masonic knowledge, stay away from "education" by using other terms. Should they use this subterfuge? I don't believe they should. I believe Conrad Hahn found this to be so in 1966. Here's the story:

What's Behind and Beyond the Ritual?

A new term, or word, has been coined. It's "Masonology." A Frenchman named Alex Mellor is its inventor. My good friend Dr. George H. T. French of Texas has carried it to further heights.

What is "Masonology?" It's a new name for good old fashioned Masonic education. It's intended to make us consider the many facets of Free-masonry—beyond the parroting of the ritual. It's another word like "culture;" "information;" "research" to get us away from that "nasty" word "education".

But, must we disguise Masonic education? Does the word "education" turn Masons away from learning something more than the ritual? I don't really think so. Let me tell you why.

For six weeks in 1966 I asked several Masonic leaders throughout the country to help me conduct a Masonic school. The officers of several lodges in my area were polled to see if enough would come to make it worthwhile. The poll was indeed heartening. The plans were made. School was started. One hundred forty men were present for the first session; 162 came for the second; the number increased each week.

At the third session the guest instructor was the late Conrad Hahn, Executive Secretary of The Masonic Service Association, and Past Grand Master of Masons in Connecticut. Here's a portion of what he had to say:

I congratulate everyone of you present here tonight. You have responded to a call, a challenge if you like, to such a degree you have really not only surprised, but made very grateful, the men who organized this kind of group meeting. You are trying to carry out a Masonic purpose. You have thereby given me some ammunition. I spent 30 years in Connecticut as a schoolmaster, and wherever I go in Masony I am told to avoid the dirty word "education" because it drives men from Masonry. Lo and behold! You have answered a call to come to school! Isn't that wonderful?

However, I note that even the Grand Lodge of Virginia labels its Committee on Education anything but education—it's a Committee on Information, Research (a dreaded word in some quarters), and Publications [since changed to Education!] In Pennsylvania it's a Committee on Masonic Culture! When I asked Bill Yeager [its Chairman and Past Grand Master] why they used the word "culture" instead of "education" he was quite frank and said: "The word education seems to drive men away." I said: "Bill, what do you think the word culture is going to do?" When I grew up in the coal mining regions of Pennsylvania culture was a word not many would confess to having had; it was something reserved for women and sissies. Education was something you had to have, like the measles. But, alas, even in Connecticut, since I left that State, the name of the Committee on Masonic Education has been changed to the Committee on Masonic Culture and Public Relations!

I'm a great believer in Masonic *Education*—I think that is the correct word—and this meeting tonight is dedicated to, and arranged for, *education*—that is, the imparting of information with the intention to bring out the best in the individuals who are concerned with the leadership of lodges here in Virginia.

The discussion tonight is centered around the words "Worshipful Master." And I might say quickly, there are many Masters, but relatively few *Worshipful* Masters. "Worshipful" means "worthy of respect". There are too many Masters who go through motions—they try hard—but they never quite grasp the meaning of the word "Worshipful" in their title. Few really work to deserve the title "worthy of respect." . . . .

Connie was speaking "off the cuff" at the session referred to above. His comments were tape recorded and transcribed. Every Mason attending the school received a copy. Some were disturbed to learn they never would be entitled to honestly be called "Worshipful"; others understood what he was saying and really earned the title.

On the statements of one of the world's truly great Freemasons I can rest my case. Masonic Education doesn't have to be disguised by newly coined words. However, it's perhaps necessary to carry this thinking a couple of steps further.

Masonic Education, I am told by another great Freemason, Dwight L. Smith of Indiana, means only the ritual in far too many areas. He feels, and so do I, that this concept must be destroyed. As I've said many times before (and long before Mellor came on the scene), Freemasonry goes far beyond the ritual. Again I'll refer to the "Body of Freemasonry" found in the first edition of *The Altar Light*. I was happy to learn several lodges enlarged that graphic presentation and posted it in their Lodges.

We learn quickly (or should) that symbolism plays an important role in Freemasonry. Symbolism and allegory covers a goodly portion of the ritual of the Craft. In fact, there are many areas that make me shudder when I have to repeat what the ritualists have made us learn. An example? The "Forty-seventh Problem of Euclid. . . ." and Pythagoras who was "raised to the sublime degree of Master Mason." This one disturbed me so much I researched the man and wrote a lengthy paper on him in 1959. But there was no way I could justify the story of him being raised to the sublime degree of Master Mason.

So, symbolism constitutes an important part of this "Body of Freemasonry." Jurisprudence does, also. This becomes evident early in the ritual of the Entered Apprentice Degree. But too often that's where it stops. Nothing further is heard about the subject unless we go searching for it. Yet, the laws of Freemasonry cover our Masonic life. We can be thrown out of the Craft for breaking the laws—the laws too many don't know exist.

We find in our ritual that benevolence is synomymous with Freemasonry. In fact, we hear this subject parroted in a portion of the ritual of the opening of every Masonic Lodge. Certainly benevolence is another important part of this Body. But what do we know about it? Outside of pleas for our Masonic Home (or other pet charity) what is taught?

The ritual, vaguely, tells us Freemasonry is a philosophy—a way of life. This important subject is truly the bloodstream of the Order. How little is taught about this most necessary subject.

Then we come to the history of Freemasonry, barely hinted at in the ritual. It is through learning the history of the Craft that we put flesh on the Body. Through the history we find everything hinted at in the ritual comes to life. Although thousands of books have been written on Freemasonry, far too often these gather dust in attics and other hard-to-get to places. A great friend and Mason often pleaded with Masons to read, read, and read some more. But they don't. At least they don't read Masonic books. Such books become "best sellers" if 5,000 are sold! And there are almost four million Masons in this country!

Masonology! Do we need a new word? I don't believe we do. But if it will help further the cause of Masonic education, I'll go along with it.

The Northeast Conference on Masonic Education and Libraries has been meeting yearly for over 30 years. It's composed of Grand Lodge representatives from Virginia eastward to Maine. Each year it meets in a different state. And each year it adopts a different theme. Because of his prominence (and perhaps because it doesn't have to pay his expenses), whoever is Executive Secretary of The Masonic Service Association is often asked to address the Conference. In 1981 Stewart M. L. Pollard gave the delegation some good and wholesome advice:

The *Grassroots* of Masonic Education

This was the topic Stewart M. L. Pollard, Executive Secretary of The Masonic Service Association selected for the Northeast Conference on Masonic Education. It met in May in Baltimore.

Pollard noted that he had been studying the work of each of the Conferences meeting throughout the country. For the past 30 years he noted "each of the conferences has addressed itself to the theme of 'Getting Back to Basics'. It's almost as though we were in competition for 're-inventing the wheel'." He found no unanimity of thought on what the basics are, or how they should be approached.

He likened the building of a Masonic life to that of building a military man. He pointed out how the two run in parallel directions. He also noted how the two must consist of continuing education. Nothing can stand still if it is to grow and accomplish a purpose.

Pollard quoted Carl Claudy as he spoke of the ritual: "After all, the ritual, no matter how valuable it may be and how necessary it is to our Lodges, is something apart from, extraneous to, the lives you and I live. We do not go to work by ritual; we do not live our social lives by Masonic ritual; we do not make love to our wives by Masonic ritual; we do not solve our problems by Masonic ritual; but by Masonic teachings."

"Ritual can be equated to the endless hours of 'close order drill' that a soldier is subjected to," said Pollard. "It is a form of discipline which assures the precision, snap and stamina exhibited on parade. It provides only periphery benefits for the soldier on the battlefield. The rote rendition of ritual, the

5

beauty of precision floor work, are only the vehicles which deliver the great truths of Masonic teachings.

"Masonic education, then, can be defined as the progressive science of translating those tenets, principles and teachings into practical application of daily living. As a progressive science, we must establish those goals (targets) based upon the knowledge and skills we have established. Just as in public education, we progress from kindergarten to primary, to elementary, to secondary and high school as our experience and skills permit, so in Masonry, we must constantly build upon our knowledge to make 'Good Men Better'."

He closed his address by suggesting four basic goals:

1. To *Brief* the candidate
2. To *Orient* the newly-initiated Entered Apprentice
3. To *Teach* the Fellowcraft
4. To *Instruct* the Master Mason

"To brief, to orient, to teach and to instruct. How basic can you get? If we accomplish this on a one-to-one basis with our new members, we can insure that the baton will be passed on."

Going back to school to learn something about what's behind the ritual has been a continuing obsession with me since I became a Master Mason. In this article I've gone a little deeper into why I believe Masonic education is a must. This is especially so if we want Freemasonry to grow.

The suggestions contained therein merely touch the tip of what can and should be done throughout the Craft. Hopefully this will cause our leadership to think of better ways and means of turning members into Master Masons.

Masonic Education?

Masonic education still appears to be something men whisper about. It's still something to be feared. It's something to ignore.

The Altar Light has been shouting about the need for Freemasons to learn something about the Craft for the past three years. I've been pleading for better methods of teaching Freemasons for over thirty years. A few others have been crying for over a century for the need of Masons to know something about Masonry. These have been too few. And for the most part they have been ignored.

For some time I've been receiving requests for my thinking on what should be done to make Master Masons instead of merely members. I don't have the answers. It appears that no one does. There are some basic steps the leadership in Freemasonry can follow, however.

In 1966, I asked the Masons in my division to go to school. For six weeks for two hour sessions they came. Each week found more participating than the week before. This caused Conrad Hahn who was the guest "teacher" for the fourth session to say: "You have proved something all Grand Lodges should be aware of. You've been asked to come to school. And you have come. You have shown all of us that 'education' isn't the dirty word we've been led to believe it is. Because some think it is they have disguised what they are attempting by calling it 'culture' or 'information' or 'research' or something other that what it really is—education."

During the six two hour sessions we discussed Masonic law, the Grand Lodge, Masonic history, Masonic philosophy, Masonic symbolism, Masonic benevolence and Masonic customs. Guest "teachers" from many areas of the country (and even England by proxie) conducted portions of each session. At the end of the course, each participant who had attended five of the six classes was presented a Grand Lodge diploma.

There must be a means of measuring the success or failure of any program. For this measurement a quiz of fifty questions was taken by each man in attendance. No names were required, just the man's rank in his Lodge. The quiz was then graded. The correct answers were read and the papers marked by the individuals, and then collected. Not surprisingly, the overall average for these precourse tests was 64% correct.

During the final hour of the final week the participants took a test on the whole course. The overall average was a whopping 96% correct. The measurement proved the "teachers" had done their job; the handouts had been studied; the men had discussed what had been taught with others in their Lodges; there were many more educated Freemasons in the area.

This wasn't a test for those who had come to school. It was a test of the principles of the teaching I had been advocating for years. I had figured most men felt as I did—that participation is the only way to learn. This was a difficult point to get across to my superiors. It had to be done to convince them, and, me. The point was proven. Everyone agreed. BUT nothing changed in the method of teaching on the level that counted—the top. Too many of us are in love with the sound of our own voices. So we continue to bore men who, in many, many cases, know more than we do by using the lecture-type of education.

At that time I'd been a member of the Grand Lodge education committee for ten years. I stuck it out for four more. Then I quit the committee to work as an individual (I'd have probably been "fired" that year anyway). Today, ten years later, the committee is still following the same methods it had for twenty-five years.

There isn't much an individual can do. But I asked the Virginia Craftsman, a traveling Masonic *degree* team to help. For years I'd been studying the principles of management. Without exception the seminars were loaded with audio-visual methods of teaching. They were not only interesting, they taught, and what was taught was retained. Why shouldn't Freemasonry use what industry had used for over twenty-five years? The Virginia Craftsmen put up enough money so a ten minute pilot film could be produced. We wanted to show the leadership of the Craft what could be done.

It didn't work. Leaders of more of the large Masonic bodies were contacted and asked to produce a series of leadership training films. None were interested. By chance, the folks at Macoy Publishing and Masonic Supply Company saw the pilot film. They decided this was one of the answers to educating Masonic leaders. They offered to invest in the production of a full length leadership film. They fully realized the company might never get its money back.

"Growing the Leader" was produced. Three Grand Lodges purchased prints. They were so enthusiastic about the results Macoy paid for the production of *"Breaking Barriers to Communication."* This led to *"Planning Unlocks the Door"* and finally *"People Make the Difference,"* a film on

organizing the Lodge and putting the proper men in the right slot for success. Last year Imagination Unlimited! purchased the rights to these films so they could be distributed through The Masonic Service Association as its contribution to a better informed Masonic leadership. Recently, Imagination Unlimited! invested in the making of new master prints so the cost of each print could be sold at a much lower price than before.

Are the training films good? The judges at the International Film and TV Festival of New York thought they were. *"The Pilot"* (remake of the original) was awarded the Silver Medal for Training Films. The other four films were entered as a series and also received a Silver Medal. No other training films for Freemasons have ever won anything in international competition.

Several Grand Lodges thought they were good. They used them along with the *Leader's Guide* to set the stage for participation during their educational and leadership workshops. Around these films they built their own programs.

Some Masonic districts have purchased the films and used them as a continuing source of education and inspiration. Many Lodges and Grand Lodges have rented varying prints. One we received no comments from; the others praised them highly.

A few weekend seminars were conducted in hotels around the state of Virginia in 1976. The program was supported by the then Grand Master and the then Director of Education. Those who attended claimed the format was what they had been searching for during their years as officers of their Lodges. They proved it with their lively participation. The only criticism was the need for many more such forums. It was pointed out that there should be films and discussions on Masonic law, symbolism, customs, the art of presiding and other such items. And there should be.

Yes, there should be. But it costs money to produce even the simplest of motion pictures. This is where the problem begins. It was pointed out graphically to me in a recent letter asking for my views on what course Masonic education should take. Cost, it was pointed out, must be a factor.

There is *nothing more expensive than ignorance*. This bears repeating over and over again. If we haven't learned this lesson yet, let's learn it right now. The events of the past few years should prove this is a true statement. We are losing members through withdrawals in overwhelming numbers. Why? Mainly because they haven't been taught the principles of Freemasonry. They haven't been taught the meaning behind the ritual—the ritual we've put on a pedestal to stagnation. We should take the ritual off the pedestal and arm it with goals, plans to reach these goals, and use of the art of communication to tell our members, and the world, what the goals and plans are.

In the first issue of *The Altar Light* there appeared a drawing to depict the *whole* body of Freemasonry. We claimed (and still do) that this body is composed of:

SYMBOLISM: the brain and heart of Freemasonry
BENEVOLENCE: Freemasonry's soul
HISTORY: The flesh for the body

JURISPRUDENCE: Its muscles
PHILOSOPHY: The body's bloodstream
RITUAL: The skeleton on which the whole body is built

The heading read: THERE CAN BE NO DEDICATION WITHOUT EDU-CATION. And there will be no dedication to Freemasonry unless we start educating our members. Parroting the ritual just isn't enough.

In that first edition I stated something that bears repeating over and over again. "We can create more problems than we solve if we send out men to teach who haven't been taught. Men must have tools with which to work or they can't do the job the way they should. This is so trite it shouldn't have to be mentioned. Perhaps it's because it's so trite that it's ignored. The basic tool is knowledge."

Along with this knowledge the Masonic teacher must be given other tools. One of the principal ones is enough money to do the job right. This brings to mind a pitiful story. Soon after the first Leadership Film was released, a good friend in charge of the educational program for a large appendant body told me he'd like to use the film. "Go ahead," I told him, "I'll help you." He shook his head, "I can't. I've only got three hundred dollars to work with!" Three hundred dollars for educating an organization of over a half-million members!

When the *Proceedings* of Grand bodies are researched we find little or nothing budgeted for education. What a contrast when you see what's budgeted for ritual. And there are those who wonder why Freemasonry is losing members through withdrawals. We wonder why good men aren't interested in becoming Freemasons.

Another tool the Masonic teacher must have is the means to make educational programs interesting; to make them "painless." This is where audio-visual teaching is important. To produce audiovisual programs costs money (as we've mentioned). Every minute saved in a production reduces the costs by hundreds of dollars. Consequently the good producer writes and rewrites his scripts. The result is a hard-hitting production that covers the story in minutes. The same story would take a lecturer hours to present. The producer uses visuals, as well as words, to save time and yet give the viewer something he will remember for years to come. It has been proven that a man remembers ten percent, or less, of what he hears; but 75% of what he *hears and sees.*

The Masonic teacher must create another tool. It's *participation.* Without participation workshops and seminars are dull. Many of us have proven to our satisfaction that participation can be achieved. With it comes remembering, excitement, enthusiasm—and the dedication. This is where audio-visual aids come in. They create the atmosphere necessary for participation. And these aids don't necessarily have to be motion pictures. Slides help. So do overhead projections. The use of simple tear pads work, also. When all of these are used in conjunction, you've got a winner.

Too often those attending Masonic workshops leave empty-handed (and perhaps empty-headed). Why not provide them with inexpensive "handouts"? These can be digests of the points covered for future study. They can be booklets from the Grand Lodge. They can include catalogs of books (Macoy Publishing and Masonic Supply Company will provide them for you). Material from The Masonic Service Association is readily available (and it, also, will provide catalogs of what it has to offer). Other leadership material is available (Imagination Unlimited! will gladly furnish you with a list of items it has for Freemasons).

Masonic education is the most vital tool in Freemasonry's arsenal. It's also the most neglected. We've considered it so vital we've been writing about it for years. Almost every issue of *The Altar Light* for three years has covered the subject. It will continue to be covered in the years ahead.

Please, let's resolve to put education to work throughout the country so we will have dedicated Master Masons.

In an early edition of The Altar Light *I touched upon the need for management in Freemasonry. Several years ago I covered the subject at more length for* The Indiana Freemason. *The subject appeared to startle some of our leadership. "Why management?" I was asked. So, I've tried to explain, my reasoning.*

Conrad Hahn, who had long known of my concerns, noted of the following article: "This is your forte. Keep on developing this department."

Freemasonry and Management

MANAGEMENT FOR FREEMASONRY? Sounds like heresay to many. But is it? Not a bit. If there hadn't been management of some nature throughout the centuries, there wouldn't be any Freemasonry today.

Our forefathers didn't call it "management," they called it "leadership," if they called it anything. It was present, though. It had to be for survival.

Usually when we think of management we think of a profit-making enterprise. And it's true that a business can't make a profit unless it has efficient management. We forget, if we've ever given it a thought, that even fraternal and voluntary organizations such as Freemasonry must make a profit. Unbelievable? No it isn't.

Actually, what is profit? It's simply income less costs—even though it isn't that simple when you make out your income tax return. In the "non-profit" organization the terminology is the same, but income becomes benefits and cost becomes unwanted considerations. So, to make a "profit" the benefits must out-weigh unwanted considerations. Do they?

Here are some benefits the members have an opportunity to receive:
- Association with good men
- Work toward charitable endeavors
- Study of the ritual, history, symbolism, philosophy
- Social activities
- Writing, speechmaking, learning to think
- Fraternalism

The Lodge must provide such benefits as:
- Recognition for its members
- Assigning responsibilities and authority to its members
- Satisfy the desire for achievement most men have

- Plan to make every meeting a **Masonic** event
- Provide excellent instruction in the ritual and all phases of Freemasonry

These are just a few of the benefits the members should receive and the Lodge should provide. Each one should be a step closer to Freemasonry's only goal—**To Make Good Men Better.** It won't be accomplished unless there is management—leadership—by the Officers of the Lodge. If we have this, we'll have a reduction in the cost factor—unwanted considerations.

Let's look at a few of these unwanted considerations to avoid:
- Sloppy degree work
- Unclean Temple, inside and out
- Smelly and dirty clothing
- Ignoring man's desire to work
- No instruction in Freemasonry
- Poorly planned meetings
- Providing nothing but degree work
- Featuring speakers who know nothing about Freemasonry

The lack of leadership has been blamed for the unwanted considerations too often found in our Lodges. The truth is, though, that we don't have a lack of leadership. The foremost leaders of every profession, industry, and trade are members. They aren't being used because there is a lack of management in our Order. Men are entering the West Gate full of vim and vigor, anxious and willing to serve the Craft. Then they leave by the East Gate disillusioned.

By not following the principles of good management (planning, communicating, organizing, staffing, controlling) we are letting potential Masonic leaders get away from us. Without efficient management we have no goals, therefore we have no leadership.

It's easy to blame "the establishment" for our own weaknesses. Everyone else is doing it, so why shouldn't we just say, "Grand Lodge isn't telling me what to do, so I'll do nothing." That's one problem. We've become conditioned to look to "Washington" for guidance. Without question, that's the sorriest thing that ever happened to the American people. For too long we've let others do our thinking for us.

We don't need Grand Lodge or "Washington" to tell us how to be good managers in Freemasonry. The first rule an efficient manager learns is that he must get things done through other people. He knows there isn't a man living who knows all there is to know about anything. He must have help. So, he puts the right man in the right slot to get the job done.

Goals must be set. They must be set by those who will be helping to achieve them. Plans must be made to reach these goals. Again, these must be established by the Team chosen to reach the goals. There must be meaningful communication to pave the way toward achieving the goals. Then there must be careful organizing, and the right men given the proper job to do. The manager will then control the action.

Examples of poor management, not only in Freemasonry, have filled volumes. When we consider the management movement, as we know it today, is relatively new, even in industry, we can't find fault because it hasn't been accepted in Freemasonry. In our Order we are slow to incorporate new ideas. This isn't bad. We have traditions, landmarks, and customs to preserve. These will not be compromised by utilizing the principles of management; they will be enhanced.

Freemasonry must continue to grow, and grow it will by using dynamic management as the key—the only key—to a stronger fulfilling, and vital Order.

What has a circus got to do with Freemasonry—or leadership? Perhaps nothing. Perhaps much. At any rate a trip to a circus caused me to view some things we do in our Fraternity in a different light. Maybe this account will do the same for you.

As I wrote the rough draft I viewed what I considered to be "The Body of Freemasonry." I passed along my thinking to Chick Larsen, not a Mason, but a top-notch artist and cartoonist. His conception has been placed on the walls of several Lodges.

The Fellow Who Does the Job

Recently I took my family to the Ringling Bros.-Barnum & Bailey Circus. This wasn't a new experience for me; it was for them. As a youngster in Pawtucket, Rhode Island, I had watered the animals and performed other odd jobs for "free" tickets. Perhaps that's why I was fascinated more by the workers than the performers the other day.

It was enlightening to watch the efficiency of the men who made the animal trainer, the acknowledged star of the show, look extremely good. Without these men who sorted out the leopards, panthers, and pumas at the proper time, there could have been chaos. Getting them back in their cages in the correct order, feeding them, cleaning up their mess, and the many other unseen tasks were just as important. All of it helped make the star the star.

The men and women who handled the ropes for the "high flying" performers; those who checked the guy wires to make certain the stars could walk on them safely; the people who manipulated the cords that raised and lowered people and props at the right time; the stage hands who quickly changed the scenes; all of these and more made the performers look good.

Without these people behind the scenes there could have been no show. In the high priced program their pictures aren't shown. Nowhere are their names listed. There are plenty of pictures of the stars and the sets. The names of the officers and heads of the production staff are displayed prominently. The people behind the scenes, the people who make the show go, are ignored.

What can this teach us about what we're doing in Freemasonry? Much. The people behind the scenes for a circus, and other profit making enterprises, do receive some satisfaction for what they are doing. They are paid to do the job. They receive something for their "non-recognition." With

17

few exceptions, this isn't true in Freemasonry, or most other non-profit organizations.

Another observation. As a consultant it is necessary for me to talk to management to determine whether or not it wants me to do a specific job. Whenever possible I try to look over the operation of the company before discussing anything with management. It seldom takes more than five minutes of watching the workers to determine just how good management is. Frequently I can quote (but certainly don't!) exactly what I'm going to hear when I sit down with the bosses. Efficiency, happiness, organization, or the lack of these, is so apparent one wonders why everyone can't see it.

Why doesn't management see what's wrong? Mainly because they live with it day by day. What is highly visible to the trained consultant isn't to those who aren't conditioned to analyze problems they have helped to create. And the disturbing thing is they usually can't see the problems until far too often it's too late to solve them without drastic action.

A good friend of mine who is in public relations, and who loves Freemasonry as I do, had this comment. "Unfortunately in Freemasonry we too often let friendship and our likes and dislikes influence us. As a leader I'm not going to give someone I don't like anything to do. He might be the best one I can find for the job, but he isn't my friend, so I'll give the job to a friend. To carry this a little farther, let's say I've just burst my appendix. In my Lodge I've got a surgeon whom I'm told is excellent. But I don't like him. We've also got a plumber whom I do like. He's my friend. He agrees with me all the time. So who do you think I'm going to have perform the operation? Why, my friend the plumber, that's who."

Unbelievable? In a way. We surely wouldn't let a plumber (or lawyer, or mortician) cut us open if we wanted to live. Yet most of us want Freemasonry to live but we're calling upon unqualified men to perform jobs of the most delicate nature. Examples are so numerous they would fill pages. So we'll just touch upon a couple at the moment.

Look at "The Body of Freemasonry" in the Frontispiece. Note the number of facets there are to keep this body healthy. As with the human body, if these parts don't function harmoniously, we're in trouble. Too often one part is favored over all others. We will find experts to work with and teach the ritual. We forsake the other parts of this Body of Freemasonry.

We create more problems than we solve if we send out men to teach who haven't been taught. Men must have tools with which to work or they can't do the job the way they should. This is so trite it shouldn't have to be mentioned. Perhaps, it's because it's so trite that it's ignored. In Freemasonry the basic tool is knowledge. The **working** tools are symbolic. Which brings us to the Body of Freemasonry as I picture it.

RITUAL—Skeleton (or framework)
SYMBOLISM—Heart and Brains
BENEVOLENCE—Soul
PHILOSOPHY—Bloodstream

18

JURISPRUDENCE—Muscles
HISTORY—Flesh (or binder)

The framework must be the ritual. It's what makes Freemasonry the distinctive Order it is. From the ritual comes the heart and brains that keeps Masonry alive and vital—its symbolism. The ritual reminds us that we must be benevolent, and that every human being has a claim upon our resources. This then becomes the soul, the conscience, of every Master Mason. Freemasonry's philosophy pumps the blood that brings life-giving qualities to the body and keeps it alive. Its jurisprudence, or laws, provides the muscles which enable the body to function fully. Its history puts flesh on the body, binding it into an unbreakable whole. This history tells us how well we've treated the body over the years.

The important question. Does Freemasonry really have something to offer to the world today? Indeed it does. But it does only if we consider the Body of Freemasonry as a whole; if we realize every part of it is important. Then the **whole** of the Order has what the world has needed, and urgently needs today and in the tomorrows. It has been vital for three centuries, possibly six. So it will be in the future, if we'll let it.

In 1981 Dwight L. Smith, then President of The Philalethes Society, started the Annual Assembly and Feast. He asked Allen E. Roberts to be the first Guest Lecturer. This paper was presented on that occasion.

Leadership: Often Sought—Seldom Attained

Leadership! Exactly what is it? Can it be developed? Or does it contain qualities that are inherited?

Thousands of similar questions have been asked many times over the years. The answers are usually cloaked in jargon few of us understand. This is unfortunate. It's unfortunate because the lack of leadership has doomed many businesses, organizations, and even governments. The lack of leadership has started every war since time began. It has caused untold suffering for man. It's the cause of much of the tumult in the world today.

The subject of leadership is so vast it would take months, even years, to discuss and develop properly. Here we can only touch upon the subject. But hopefully a point or two can be brought out that you will dwell on in the months ahead.

Why have I chosen this subject for this particular occasion? There are some beautiful, philosophical subjects I could cover. One or two might even make me popular (perhaps).

Quite frankly, I'm disturbed. I'm disturbed because, fortunately or unfortunately, I love Freemasonry. It has occupied most of my whole adult life. It has done this because I firmly believe it's the one organization in existence that can bring about the Brotherhood of Man under the Fatherhood of God throughout the world. But it can do it only under enlightened, knowledgeable, dedicated Masonic leadership. I emphasize Masonic leadership.

The Philalethes Society is composed of thinking, interested, dedicated, and reading Master Masons. For more than 25 years I've attended these meetings of the little bodies of Freemasons who meet here each year. You come usually at your own expense. You are the heart and soul of the Craft. You are the men who are, or will be, leading Freemasonry in many parts of our country, and even overseas. You are the men who should be bringing out the full potential of Freemasonry.

21

Over the years many of these meetings of The Philalethes Society were actually workshops. We met to impart and receive more knowledge about Freemasonry. Some of these workshops were outstanding. They left us with a burning desire to go back to our Lodges and put them to work. This met with some success—for a short time. But the fire that was kindled too often sputtered and died. The fire was put out by a leadership that couldn't tolerate success.

Last year our President decreed these annual meetings should go a step further. They have become Annual Feasts. For one, I applaud this step back to the 18th century. I'll have more to say about this later.

This year our President has added another step. There is now a Philalethes Society Lecturer on the agenda. His plan is a good one—though his choice for the first one will be questioned by many of you.

Last year a giant step was taken at the Annual Feast. There was an attempt to identify an Ideal Lodge. How desperately we need these! For over 30 years I've searched for that Ideal Lodge. I'll continue to search.

On several occasions I've thought I found one. What I found turned out to be a whisp of brilliant light—a light that glowed, only to be dimmed and shattered.

What caused the brilliance? A good, determined leader. Why was the light shattered? Because the leader died, moved to other climes, or wasn't allowed to lead any longer.

The latter has happened most often. Why? Why in the world would a good leader be suppressed? Why would he be kept from building, especially in this Society of "Builders"?

There are many answers. You know those answers. I fear a few of you have helped to destroy some of these leaders, unwittingly, or deliberately.

I don't know all the answers, so I can't develop them. No man does know all the answers. There are some who think they do. This becomes one of the biggest reasons good leaders often aren't allowed to lead. The fellow in charge knows everything about all things. He's certainly not going to let anyone appear to be better than he is. No one's going to outshine him!

There's no better way than this to keep an organization stagnant—or kill it. In the days ahead you might supply some of the many reasons why good leaders are destroyed. Then you may help Freemasonry to grow.

Without question, leadership is what Freemasonry must have at every level. This is true for any organization. With knowledgeable, dedicated leadership there's no limit to what can be accomplished.

But where are we going to find these leaders?

First, let's destroy the myth that the qualities of leadership are inherited. They are not. They must be developed. It takes hard work and determination to acquire these qualities. Yet, leaders can be found everywhere. But, a word of caution. Not all of them should be pushed to the top.

The "Peter Principle" is just as prevalent in Freemasonry as it is in government and industry. Lawrence F. Peters claims: "In every hierarchy each employee tends to rise to the level of his incompetence." Think on that statement for a few moments.

Except under unusual circumstances, a worker starts with a vocation. As he becomes proficient, he climbs up the ladder of responsibility. The further up the ladder he goes, the less vocational work he's supposed to do; the more managerial duties he must perform. If he reaches the top, 100% of his time, thoughts, and actions must be devoted to management. This means the vocational work of previous years must be ignored.

Not many men can survive this change. An excellent salesman, an outstanding engineer, a fine lawyer doesn't necessarily mean a promotion to management is in the best interests of the man or organization. In fact, too often it proves disastrous. There are classic examples all around us.

How does this relate to Freemasonry? What's the first thing we encounter when we're accepted into the Craft? The ritual. What's the only thing we're forced to learn about Freemasonry? The ritual. What's the one thing stressed throughout our Masonic careers? The ritual. What's the one thing we must understand if we want to become Worshipful Master? The ritual.

Sounds like a broken record, doesn't it? The needle has been stuck in this groove for centuries. In many jurisdictions, including mine, the ritualists determine who will become the leaders of the Lodges. This also determines who will become the leaders in the Grand Lodges.

Is this the way it should be? No, Sir. And it isn't lawful, either. Not if you believe in following the supreme law of Freemasonry—The Constitutions. Here's what they say in Article IV, of 'Masters, Wardens, Fellows and Apprentices?' "All Preferment among Masons is grounded upon real Worth and personal Merit only; that so the Lords may be well served, the Brethren not put to shame, nor the Royal Craft dispis'd: Therefore no Master or Warden is chosen by Seniority, but for Merit." You be the judge of what that statement means.

A good ritualist doesn't necessarily make a good leader. Far too often this is the "Peter Principle" at work. Far too often the good ritualist is elevated to his "level of incompetency." He, and those under him suffer, and Freemasonry is damaged. What has happened to "Merit" when this happens?

Can we blame a man who has spent countless hours in perfecting the learning of the catechisms and lectures for not wanting to give them up? Should we expect him to put aside this feeling of security? Can we expect him to devote more time to leadership, or management, as he goes through the line? Should he give up this "crutch" called "the ritual" which he has to lean on?

What's the solution? There are several. Some I can think of and there are many more you can cover.

First, the system can be changed so the qualities of leadership must be considered before a man can be elected to the line in our Lodges. It could be made mandatory for a man to throughly understand the many facets of Freemasonry. It isn't too much to ask a potential leader to understand the philosophy of the Order. He should be taught that symbolism and benevolence are important. At the least, he should know the laws of his Grand Lodge. He should be made to prove his knowledge of these, and other Masonic subjects.

Realistically, this isn't about to happen. The ritualists control Freemasonry and they aren't about to let go. Even so, we can still have excellent leadership in our Lodges, Grand Lodges, and other Masonic bodies. It may not be at the top, but it must come from there. The ritualists can remain in control, but delegate the activities of the Craft to those who understand what leadership is.

For more than 30 years I've had a sign over my desk which reads: "There's no limit to what you can accomplish, if you don't care who gets the credit." It's surprising to find how often this philosophy works.

Where are we going to find these leaders we've been discussing? I'll not burden you with what to look for in a leader, or a potential leader. You can find the criteria in any good book on management. Even my book, *Key To Freemasonry's Growth,* covers the subject. Let me point out some things here that you may not readily find anywhere else, unless you're willing to spend a couple of thousand dollars.

All of you are familiar with Abraham H. Maslow's five steps in behavioral patterns. Briefly they begin with man's basic needs: food, clothing, shelter, money. His next step becomes the need for safety and economic security. Usually a man has met these needs before he petitions a Masonic Lodge. So the next three steps are important if we want Freemasonry to grow.

Freemasonry must meet his social and ego needs. It must try to help his self-esteem and help him realize his self-fulfillment requirements. If it does, he can reach the pinacle of Maslow's hierarchy—self-realization.

Here's another concept that follows, yet goes beyond, Maslow's theory. It has been developed by Professor Clare W. Graves who has made a life-long study of human behavior. He believes there are at least seven levels of human behavior. Because these will take some digesting. I've prepared a summary of them for you to take with you to chew on. It's part of the $2,000 I mentioned.

Level one Graves terms autistic. Here man's energies are almost all consumed just trying to stay alive. He is aware of little more than the problems of sustenance: illness, reproduction, disputes. He thinks and often reacts as an animal. To manage him, one must use raw, naked force, and then can only expect limited production from him. There are still far, far too many existing on this level.

Level two brings a man a step higher. His brain is beginning to awaken and he's becoming aware of his existence as a person. This level is termed egocentric. This man is concerned only with "me." He quickly learns how to become a manipulator. He conceives ways to benefit "me" and "to hell with thee." He believes the victor gets the spoils and "might is right." He believes authority has the right to use any force necessary, firing, excommunication, or killing. To manage him, one must use exploitation, yet moderate it with sensitivity and reasonable compassion.

Absolutistic is the third level, and usually the first of concern to Freemasonry. At this level, Professor Graves has found, most men won't respond to independence and participation. They would rather have autocracy than democracy. They believe one is what one is born to be. Everything has been prescribed and laid down by some extra-human power. They live in a "moralistically prescribed world." Rigid rules must be established and enforced if they are to be managed successfully.

The fourth level is termed objectivistic. Here man believes in the power of self. He believes he can alter the established order through the exercise of his own will. He isn't about to fit into any prescribed organizational design. He believes that he is right, and it's his right to change anything to his own desires. All who disagree with him are wrong, and are simply submitting to rules made by the favored few. He can work with those on lower levels, but feels threatened by those on his own or higher levels. His real battle is for power, not material gain. In many respects he's no better than those on the second level, just brainier. To manage him, one must realize it's difficult, but take into account he's more interested in power than material gain.

Sociocentric is the term for level five. Here man becomes more concerned about social than material matters. As a manager, or leader, he shows some concern for production and for people. His social needs are more important to him than work. When both the manager and producer are on this level, participative management must be the objective. This fifth level person doesn't believe that hard work is necessary to prove anything, nor is it his moral duty to do his best. He is "group-minded." This can be dangerous. He is more interested in group-decision-making than letting one man be responsible for the growth or death of an organization. He is prone to waste time by consistently holding one meeting after another, thereby accomplishing nothing. Participation and goal-setting are necessary to manage him.

Common fears won't motivate the problemistic, or sixth level man. He doesn't fear God, boss, or social disapproval. He is confident of his own ability and capacity to survive, no matter what happens. He is end-oriented, not means-oriented. He won't be told how to do his work. He feels it's his job to get the task done, not how to do it in a particular way. He believes management should provide the tools to do the job, then he should be left alone to do the organizing and get the job done. Management can work with him in setting goals, but it must not prescribe the manner in which he reaches them.

Here's where we run into problems in Freemasonry. There are many members on this level. There are also many Masonic leaders on lower levels. The lower level leaders tend to squeeze the sixth level member out. If this doesn't succeed, they will bury him. His talent is lost. His creative excellence is destroyed by this short-sighted leadership, and all because he won't conform to the "common mold." Those who follow this type of leadership are too often the mediocre ones who are willing to conform to what the leader considers orthodox. Yet, the wise manager will take advantage of this man. The leader will use participation in setting goals, then leave the man alone to reach those goals.

Intuitionistic is the term Graves uses for the seventh level person. He's a "softened version of the sixth level man." He's still end-oriented, but he doesn't fight, per se. He does insist on an atmosphere of trust and respect, and he will avoid any type of relationship in which others try to dominate him. He must be approached through management which takes into account that he is competent and responsible. He must be supported in the things he does. He won't subordinate his desires to those of the organization. He'll simply wait for the leadership to change, while he retires into "another world." Usually he'll continue to do a passable job. When the opportunity arrives, he'll quietly attempt to have the changes made he believes necessary. Again, the wise manager will welcome this man with open arms, accept him as he is, support him, let him use his competence and responsibility to make the "boss" look good.

Many men in Freemasonry are a mixture of one or more of these levels. Good leaders will take this into account in their evaluation.

Why have I discussed human behavior with you? Because, as I mentioned earlier, I'm disturbed. We, the rank and file Master Masons, are looking to our leaders for inspiration. We are seeking information about the Craft. We're looking for many things we aren't getting.

You and I are among a privileged few. We are Master Masons. We belong to the greatest fraternal organization ever created. We have an opportunity to turn the world around and make all men act as brothers. We can't do it unless we have Constructive Leadership. We can't have Constructive Leadership unless this leadership understands human behavior. Without it, the Ideal Lodge will remain elusive.

Earlier I applauded this idea of an Annual Feast for The Philalethes Society. Why? I believe one of the Qualities the Ideal Lodge and the Ideal Leader must provide for the members is—fun.

Now, I'm not talking about Tomfoolery. I'm talking about special banquets, family affairs, Table Lodges, musicals, plays, and other cultural events for the members, and for the general public. I'm talking about getting back to the days of our forefathers who weren't afraid to laugh, to have fun. I'm referring to the days before the "do-gooders" of the middle 1800's won their battle to abolish laughter, feasting, and all types of harmless fun.

You'll also note I've mentioned setting goals and participation. If we're to have Ideal Lodges, we must have leaders who know how to set goals. Have you ever tried to accomplish anything of importance without first setting a goal? If you have, you know it's virtually impossible.

If you're asked to give a talk, you must set goals for that talk. If you plan a Lodge dinner, you'll have to set many goals or find it doomed to failure. So it goes with anything you want to accomplish. You must set goals.

Along with goals comes planning to reach them. Plans are all-important. The best way to develop plans to reach our goals is through participation. We must have the cooperation of those who will work with us. The best way to get this is through participation. The Ideal Leader knows this. He knows his goals are important only to himself. People are only committed to achieve those goals they help to set.

The Ideal Lodge must have an Ideal Leader who will use the other principles of good management. Besides goal setting and planning, these include communicating, staffing, organizing and controlling.

The Ideal Lodge can have the best goals and follow well laid plans, but these must be communicated properly or nothing will be accomplished. The right men must be placed in the proper slots, or little will be gained. The whole project must be competently organized, and controls must be determined and followed, if there is to be success.

You're aware as I am that I've only touched upon the many attributes necessary for a Constructive Leader and an Ideal Lodge. As I mentioned earlier, it would take months to develop this important subject. And I firmly believe we should waste not another minute in developing, and growing the Masonic leaders we must have today and the many tomorrows to come.

Today I wouldn't change a word I wrote in 1969 in *Key To Freemasonry's Growth*. I would, however, enlarge upon what's written there. Even so, the ending would remain the same:

> Among the rocks there is plenty of fertile ground and the seeds for Freemasonry's growth are abundant. All it will take is work to till the soil. Constructive Leaders can be found anywhere who are more than willing and anxious to grab a hoe. The present leadership must furnish the tools.

Good management is the key to Freemasonry's growth. May it be put to work.

Here's a brief outline of the human behavioral steps Professor Graves developed

1. Autistic
   Man's energy is almost consumed in the process of staying alive; his basic physical needs are all important.
   To manage: Use raw, naked force.
2. Egocentric
   Man's brain is awakening after his physical needs are met; becomes concerned about "me"; becomes a manipulator.
   To manage: Exploit, but use sensitivity and reasonable compassion.
3. Absolutistic
   Man chooses autocratic rather than democratic methods; doesn't believe in participation; lives in a moralistically prescribed world. To manage: Establish and enforce rigid rules.
4. Objectivistic
   Believes in his own power; "knows" he can alter established power by his own will; believes he's right, others wrong.

To manage: Realize it's difficult, but take into account he's out for power, not material gain.

5. Sociocentric

He's concerned with social, not material matters; is concerned for people and production; his social needs are more important than work; is group-minded. To manage: Use participation and group decision-making insofar as possible.

6. Problemistic

He doesn't fear God, boss, or social disapproval; he's confident he can survive no matter what happens; believes in participation and goals. To manage: Use participation and goal-setting.

7. Intuitionistic

He's end, not means, oriented; insists on trust and respect; won't be dominated; won't subordinate his desires to those of the organization. To manage: Accept him as he is; be supportive; accept the fact that he's competent and responsible. He's the man to have on your side!

Professor Graves cautions against managers on a lower level burying the creativity and talent of the workers on higher intellectual levels.

It is well to remember those on a higher level can make the boss look much better than he really is, if the boss will let them.

It's also good to remember: "There's no limit to what you can accomplish, if you don't care who gets the credit."

Abraham H. Maslow's theory of behavioral patterns as outlined in *Key To Freemasonry's Growth:*

The needs for the worker in Freemasonry are different than from the worker in industry. But if the basic needs; money, food, clothing, shelter; are not adequately acquired from employment, the organization will often suffer . . .

Fortunately, most of those who enter Freemasonry have met their basic needs. The Fraternity must supply their social and ego needs, because if they did not have those, it is doubtful that they would be Freemasons . . . Freemasonry has a golden opportunity to enrich the lives of these men.

Status is something everyone with a degree of ambition seeks . . .

All men have a need to satisfy their egos. All men want an opportunity to satisfy their self-esteem and a chance for self-fulfillment. The degree will vary with the individual, but the more ambitious he is, the more his ego must be satisfied, or the organization will be the loser. Subordinates always believe they posses valuable information that will be useful to those in command. And many times they are correct! They should be given an opportunity to state their views. Their recommendations and experience, when treated with respect, will help satisfy their ego needs . . .

Those few men who have a strong need for self-fulfillment are, almost without exception, creative. They are constantly visualizing new ideas. Most of the time the ideas are practical.

From *Key to Freemasonry's Growth* by Allen E. Roberts, Copyright 1969; Macoy Publishing and Masonic Supply Company, Richmond, Va.

At each seminar I conduct, if there's an overhead projector, I put on the screen a cartoon. It depicts a fellow jumping up and down crying: "It can't be done!" We then open the session by getting the reaction about what this means. Unfortunately, it doesn't mean anything to many of those in attendance. It does tell a few, though, that once you say "It can't be done," it can't.

As I've noted in what follows, it was also the title of the address I made at the end of the Northeast Conference in 1968. The full text became a Short Talk Bulletin *of The Masonic Service Association, and was reproduced in* Key to Freemasonry's Growth.

If you believe I'm obsessed with the idea that anything can be done, you're correct. But one thing you'll learn from these pages is that I know that no one man has all the answers. In those seminars I mentioned eyebrows raised when I claim: "Everyone in this room knows something that no one else in this room knows." It didn't take long to prove this point. So, while something may be needed that I can't do, there's someone who can.

It Can Be Done!

In 1968, William A. Carpenter, then Librarian of the Grand Lodge of Pennsylvania, and Executive Secretary of the Northeast Conference on Masonic Education (now a past Grand Master), asked me to tell the Conference how we could make Master Masons life-long active members. A big order, indeed.

At first I refused the assignment. There are men much better qualified than I to take on that task. But Bill insisted, and if you know him you know he's a hard man to refuse.

What I developed for that Conference became a *Short Talk Bulletin* of The Masonic Service Association in 1968 entitled "We Can Do It!" It also became Appendix I of *Key to Freemasonry's Growth.* Since 1969 when the book was first published many of the items I mentioned in this talk have been stressed, and sometimes put into practice, in several areas. But far, far too often what is advocated there is ignored.

Would I change anything I wrote in that talk or that book today? This is a question I've been asked several times. Nope. If anything, I'd try to be more emphatic.

Basically, what I claimed then still holds true. There can be NO DEDICA-TION WITHOUT EDUCATION. You can't become a plumber unless you've served an apprenticeship and learned what plumbing is all about. You can't become a doctor or lawyer, or anything else in the professions, without years of study.

You can't make a Masonic editor of a newspaper employee unless he has studied Freemasonry for years. Yet this is just what's happening in many areas. You can't take a college professor and turn him loose as a Masonic educator unless he has an extensive background in the many facets of Freemasonry. He may be a whiz in teaching Shakespeare or engineering, but these are way off the mark in Masonry. Because you're a friend of the Worshipful Master or Grand Master doesn't mean you're going to be a Masonic writer or Masonic teacher. It takes much more than friendship to understand what the philosophy of Freemasonry is.

Recently a minister spoke at a rededication breakfast held annually by two Lodges. After telling us more than we really wanted to know about King Solomon's Temple, he closed by claiming the world is in a terrible mess. Masonry is also in a terrible mess, he said, mainly because it has no purpose for existing. It should be fighting communism he felt. And this appeared to be what he would have for the Craft's purpose for existing.

This minister is a fine fellow. He knows his Bible. He keeps up with the world events. He is really a brilliant person. But he knows absolutely nothing about Freemasonry. I won't go into the many reasons why I know this is true. For one thing, if he knew even a little about Freemasonry he would know it does fight communism.

During the Grand Masters Conference in 1939 a "Declaration of Principles" was adopted. This opened by stating: "Freemasonry is a charitable, benevolent, educational society. Its principles are proclaimed as widely as men will hear. Its only secrets are in its methods of recognition and of symbolic instruction." Read that again. I've been condemned by a couple of fellows for claiming there are no secrets in Freemasonry.

The Declaration ended with this: "It further affirms its conviction that it is not only contrary to the fundamental principles of Freemasonry, but dangerous to its unity, strength, usefulness and welfare, for Masonic Bodies to take action or attempt to exercise pressure or influence for or against any legislation, or in any way to attempt to procure the election or appointment of government officials, or to influence them, whether or not members of the Fraternity, in the performance of their official duties. The true Freemason will act in civil life according to his individual judgment and the dictates of his conscience."

Now that declaration goes along with what our founding fathers, in their great wisdom decreed—keep religion, politics, race, and anything else that divides men out of Masonic Lodges.

But here's the kicker that our minister Mason didn't know. In 1948 the Declaration had this added: "Masonry abhors communism as being repugnant to its conception of the dignity of the individual personality, destructive of the basic rights which are the Divine Heritage of all men and inimical to the fundamental Masonic tenet of faith in God."

All right. Although he didn't know it, Freemasonry does "abhor communism," and rightly so. But should this be a purpose for Freemasonry's existence? How far would the Fraternity have come after 1717 if its purpose for existing was simply to "abhor" anything? Would this have made it the largest, and oldest, fraternal organization the world has ever known? I don't think so. Being an "againer" doesn't make a "doer."

It can be done! We can do it! We can get Freemasonry's message across and make every *Master Mason* a life-long active member. But we first must make them *Master Masons*. This isn't accomplished simply by conferring three degrees. These are only the beginning. It's the beginning of a life-long journey into the many aspects of the Fraternity.

For over 30 years I've been stressing the need for *knowledgeable, dedicated* Masonic leadership. We're finding this in isolated cases. Many of them have been reported in the pages of *The Altar Light*. But I fear too often the cry for training Masonic leaders is really hypocritical.

Some time ago a leading publication supported by a Grand Lodge printed a beautiful reason for training leaders in Freemasonry. It was written by the Grand Master. I wrote an article for the magazine which was never published. Its title: "Masonic leaders: Do we really want them?" If we do, we can find them. But a real leader isn't always the most popular man around. He's going to call a spade a spade; he's not going to let his "boss" lose the ball and end up looking like a fool. He won't be a "yes" man.

We can turn around much of the apathy pervading the Craft. We can do it by giving our members some of the things they are finding in appendant bodies. To do this we must have Masonic leaders willing to get off their hands to think and work.

Freemasonry, thank God, is still an organization of individuals. If we will give these individuals an opportunity to work for the Order we'll be amazed at what can happen. If we'll let these individuals participate in all that Masonry has to offer, we'll find the Craft growing by leaps and bounds.

It can be done! Let's do it.

After the BIG war had ended I settled in Virginia and wanted to become a Free-mason. I had been impressed by the Masons I had known at sea and at Chief's school in San Diego. My wife worked for a "32⁰ Mason." I asked him how I could be a member. He said he would get back with me. Six months went by and I heard nothing from him. When I talked to him again he admitted he didn't know what to tell me.

A short time later I moved to Highland Springs and changed my church affiliation. One Sunday morning I said to a friend whom I knew to be a Mason: "I've always wanted to be a Mason, John, but I reckon Masons don't like me."

"What makes you say that?" John asked. "None of you have ever asked me to join," I answered. He laughed, "And none of us ever will. But you've asked, so I'll see what I can do." That afternoon I had a petition. Two years after I'd asked how I could become a Mason!

An isolated case? No, indeed. The same thing is happening every day—even in this "enlightened" age. Too many know so little about Freemasonry they are afraid to talk about it to anyone. They're afraid of giving away our "secrets." That's the reason for the item that follows.

There Are No Secrets
In Freemasonry

(Note: On May 11, 1979, I was the keynote speaker for the triennial Regional Masonic Workshops held in Guelph, Ontario, Canada. What I said wasn't written, so what follows may not be exactly what I said then. But it will be close.

There are no secrets in Freemasonry. That's a statement I made several years ago—not in a talk—but in an off-the-cuff remark to something said in a Masonic workshop. The gasps were audible. I heard from several old-timers after the session was over. I didn't elaborate on my statement then, and never have until now. But I've thought about it often.

Actually, what secrets do we really have in Freemasonry? Is its purpose for existence concealed? Yes it is—but it shouldn't be. So let me uncover it now. Freemasonry's only purpose for existence is to accept good men into its membership and help to make them better. Freemasonry is simply a way of life.

Does this mean all Freemasons are good men and those who don't belong aren't? No, indeed! We all know many men who shouldn't be Masons. By the same token we all know many men who should be. I like this statement made by a man whom I consider to be one of the greatest servants of God, Joseph Fort Newton, D.D.: "Freemasonry's simplicity, its dignity, and its spirituality sustain me in all that I try to do, and *permit me to forget the incredible pettiness of mind that we sometimes encounter,* sustaining and enabling me to join hands with my Brethren everywhere, to do something, if it be only a little, before the end of the day, to make a gentler, kinder, and wiser world in which to live."

Those words were spoken by that gentle man during a particularly stormy session of the Masonic Service Association; a time when many of the leaders of Freemasonry were practicing anything but what they had been taught in their Lodges.

And it's no secret that we don't put into practice all the time the tenets, of our Order: Brotherly Love, Relief and Truth. Often we'll forget the Cardinal Virtues, Temperance, Fortitude, Prudence, and Justice. These are the things we stand for. They shouldn't be hidden from the world.

The lack of leadership in Freemasonry isn't hidden. It's openly discussed in the *Proceedings* of almost every Grand Lodge. It has been a plea of many real Masonic leaders since the formation of a Grand Lodge in England in 1717 (and I suspect it was a problem of our operative Brethren hundreds of years earlier). Here's what James Anderson had to say about leadership in the *Constitutions* adopted in 1723:

"All Preferment among *Masons* is grounded upon real Worth and personal Merit only; that so the *Lords* may be well served, the Brethren not put to Shame, nor the *Royal Craft* despis'd: Therefore no *Master or Warden* is chosen by Seniority, but for his Merit."

I don't think I'm revealing any secret when I say this wise counsel hasn't always been followed. But if it had been, how much better our Craft would be today. And it's wisdom like this that has caused me to revere our founding fathers.

Whose fault is it because the lack of leadership is deplored? Everyone points his finger at some other person. The top blames the bottom; the bottom blames the top. As in every case there are three sides: His, mine, and somewhere in between the real reason. There are those who claim I'm wrong; there are only two sides. But I've always found three.

Isn't it time though, for us to stop pointing fingers and go about the task of building leadership? Isn't it time we started searching for Masons who know more than we do? One of the greatest faults I've found almost everywhere is the leadership's fear of the men who really do a job. Far too often we forget, if we've given it a thought, that no man knows all the answers to anything. I try to shy away from those who think they do.

Each of us knows something that no one else knows. Each of us has a vast amount of knowledge about one or more particular things—more so, perhaps, than anyone else. Bringing this knowledge together and working as a team, or series of teams, there is absolutely no limit to what we can accomplish.

This subject could be expanded on indefinitely, but let's go to another subject that has a bearing on leadership. This is Masonic literature. I don't know about you, but I have learned more from reading than from any other way. Freemasonry is supposed to be a school—a college—of sorts. It certainly was for our operative Brethren. Every Masonic Lodge, and Grand Lodge, should have vast libraries of Masonic books and other literature. But they don't. Rare indeed is the Lodge that has any type of reading material for its members.

It's certainly no secret that Freemasons, as a whole, aren't READERS. Over the years there have been several publishers of Masonic books. Today there are few. There is only one I know about. It has absorbed many of the others forced out of business. Why?

Did you know that a Masonic book selling 5,000 copies becomes a Masonic best-seller? Amazing, isn't it? Especially when you consider there are well over four million card-carrying members in the United States and Canada. And with the cost of publishing books today, any production under 5,000 copies makes the cost prohibitive. This will result, and already has, in the publication of even fewer Masonic books than in the past. As an author I've been fortunate. Each of my books has passed the magical figure.

It's no secret that this lack of readership has caused a lack of management in our Lodges. I strongly favor audio-visual education, and this includes the teaching of management. This system will work wonders when properly used. We've proved it over and over again. Yet, Freemasonry, which should be the first to try new methods, is reluctant to incorporate what private industry, and even the backward thinking governments have been using for a quarter century. But even with audio-visual training, it must be supplemented by reading. There will always be a need for literature. But no literature is going to help those who don't read it.

Is there anyone today who doesn't believe public relations is important? Is there anyone who doesn't know every organization has a public image? I can't believe there is. But it should be no secret that Freemasonry's public image is somewhat vague. Most people outside our Order (and even too many within it) know nothing about us, and they could care less. Periodically some reporter or article writer will attempt to tell the public about Freemasonry. And they don't treat us kindly. We become "weirdoes," "racists," "boozers," "murderers," "torturers." The list goes on and on.

Why? Why do we permit the public to be bombarded with these lies about the Craft? Mainly because Freemasonry, as a whole, has let these statements go unchallenged. We have done this, I fear, because we don't know how to answer them.

Two Grand Lodges that I know about had top-notch Public Relations committees. They functioned in one case for three years, in another five. The public in those states learned something of the good Freemasonry does while these committees were active. Then, for some unknown reason, the committees were abolished. The progress made was lost, and the momentum will probably never be regained.

Internal relations are as important as outside relations. Far too often we ignore this reality. We must include our ladies in our events. We must bring together those of our members who aren't interested in the ritual. We can do this by providing interesting programs for them several times each year. Only good taste dictates the type of programs the Lodges can provide. There is no limit to the number of imaginative events that can be shared by everyone.

Once the program is determined, don't hide it. Promote it. Advertise it. Let the membership know about it. But this should be true of everything the Lodge does. A monthly newsletter, not a mere postcard, not a bulletin filled with names and titles, should be a must with every Lodge. The members, even those who don't attend, should be kept fully informed about what the Lodge has done and will do. This simple internal relations activity will be welcomed. And who knows, it just might boost the attendance; it certainly will the interest.

By practicing internal relations, we just might keep Masonic-related bodies from sapping the strength of the Lodge. Or, as Dwight Smith of Indiana puts it, we may be able to keep Masonic-related bodies from killing the goose that laid the golden egg. Far too often the foundation—the lodge—is forgotten by these bodies depending upon Master Masons for their existence. And whose fault is it? Again fingers are pointed. But again we should put the fingers down, roll up our sleeves, and go to work.

Some of our Masonic-related bodies are providing Freemasons with opportunities for work and fun. Some of these things our Lodges should be providing. In 1968 I told an educational conference in Vermont that "We Can Do It!" We can make *Master Masons* life-long active members. But only if we make them *Master Masons*—not merely members. Only if we provide knowledgeable leadership. Only if we give every Master Mason an opportunity to do what he wants to do.

Let me emphasize something now that I hinted at then. I did emphasize it in my audio-leadership course, along with several other things I've merely touched on here. This point is merely one word—FUN. But what a word it is! It's the key to the success of every Lodge, every organization. If attending Lodge is drudgery, there won't be many in attendance. If it's fun, members and visitors will be present from miles around. Fun is what we've got to have in Masonry. We've got to make it something to enjoy.

Let me hasten to add I don't mean undignified tomfoolery. I mean a sharing of philosophical values in such a way it leaves everyone with a sense of well-being. Or, as the late Conrad Hahn put it: "Masons should radiate the joy of wisdom."

Our founding fathers designed Freemasonry to be fun. Unfortunately, this concept was changed in later years. But in those Lodges today where their concept is followed, there is growth because there is warmth and fellowship.

Let's let this warmth and fellowship beam out to our homes, our jobs, our churches, and our communities.

We'll do this, and have fun at the same time, if we'll really look at the whole "Body of Freemasonry." To me this consists of Ritual, Symbolism, Benevolence, Philosophy, Jurisprudence, and History. You'll note I consider this "Body" consists of six parts—not one, as far too many do. The Ritual isn't all there is to Freemasonry. It's important. It's the "skeleton" on which the rest of the "body" is formed.

Symbolism is the heart and brains of this body. It keeps Freemasonry alive and vital. *Benevolence* is the soul. Through our ritual and symbolism we find every human being has a claim upon every Master Mason. The *Philosophy* of Freemasonry is its bloodstream. It pumps the blood with life-giving qualities keeping the body alive and active. *Jurisprudence,* or law, provides the muscles enabling the body to function fully. Without this jurisprudence there would be chaos. *History* puts flesh on the body. It binds it into an unbreakable whole. It tells us how well we've treated the body over the years. It tells us how we should treat it in the future.

Through my study of this "Body" over the years, I've concluded Freemasonry still has much to offer the world today. Freemasonry has what the world has always needed. That's love, compassion, justice, and everything else that's positive. Actually, what it has to offer, and what the world desperately needs, can be summed up in one word—*Brotherhood.*

Many points have been covered here. And if I was to sum them up and be asked which I considered the most important I would say—*Internal and Public Relations.* You will note I've put Internal Relations first. This is deliberate. Through enlightened leadership we can turn members into Master Masons. Through education we can have dedication. This dedication will bring into the forefront everything I've talked about here—and more.

Please remember this, even if you forget everything else I've said: No one can be dedicated to something he knows nothing about. Education will bring dedication to the principles of Freemasonry. And that's no secret.

But we do have secrets I've been told. A couple of grips and a couple of words—and. . . . They aren't secrets. Go to any large book store or library. You'll find them in print. There are no secrets in Freemasonry.

Only once in five years did I let someone speak for me under "Viewpoints," our editorial column. It was taken from an address by F. K. Knox of New Zealand, which was reproduced in the **Freemason** of New Zealand. He became a Mason in 1947, was Worshipful Master in 1959. He held several offices in Grand Lodge before he was elected Grand Master. He served in the Royal Navy and the Royal New Zealand Navy from 1938 to 1946. He is a professional accountant; holds a degree in Commerce; was district manager for a large insurance company; was a stock and share broker. He still serves in many charitable organizations, in addition to working for Freemasonry.

It's always good to get someone else's viewpoint, especially when it's much the same as your's. What he has to say is something all Masonic leaders should evaluate.

There's A Place for Freemasonry

If Freemasonry is locked away in our lodge rooms it will become as expressive as the furniture—beautiful but dumb. To be effective, Freemasonry needs to be practiced by its adherents not so much by word as by example. Its teachings must first capture the imagination, be accepted in our hearts as worthy of time and thought and then finally be translated into a way of life which will govern and colour our every decision.

It is the practice of this Masonic way of life that we project the external image that Masons are men of probity, or integrity and of good character.

And it is only when the community at large can see that Freemasonry has a beneficial influence on men that we will bring worthy citizens to our door.

The Craft is in competition for the minds and the time of men. . . . The first requisite if we are to survive and resume our former pattern of steady growth is a willingness to face and adapt to change. It is a well-known truism that the fate of a living species which fails to adapt to changes in environment is death.

And so it has been throughout history for organizations, nations, and whole civilizations. They rise, flourish and decay, leaving behind scant evidence of their one-time power and influence. . . .

I sincerely believe that there is a place, and a place of growing importance, for the teaching of Freemasonry in the permissive society. Young, thinking people are searching for spiritual signposts in an uncertain world and those who are prepared to accept the discipline of our moral philosophies could well find their answers in Freemasonry. Certainly we have nothing to be ashamed of. . . .

For too long we have lived in the shadows, content to be an introverted society. We can no longer afford that luxury if we are to survive. We must as a matter of great urgency adopt a more positive attitude toward new members and in particular let our own membership realize that to function the Craft urgently needs candidates. It requires younger men to carry us to the future.

I am not saying that we should give away the landmark which insists that a potential candidate take the first step. What I am trying to say is that we must not lose the opportunities to fan the flame of interest when a friend has expressed the first tentative interest in joining. . . .

We must be prepared to a certain extent to come out into the open and suffer the scrutiny of the world from where the young men we require will come. . . .

We should be prepared to adopt the modern techniques of professional public relations people to ensure that Freemasonry receives a favourable projection of its image—to be seen as an organization which can and does work for the good of society and not as a secret organization with a rather subversive aura. . . .

We should not shrink from an examination of outdated customs. In particular, we should be prepared to follow and adopt new trends conceived by sister constitutions, encourage the formation of daylight lodges, permit our lodges to experiment with variable meeting times, perhaps permit a wider discretion of the question of acceptable dress, involve our wives and families a great deal more in our social activities and, above all, live openly in the community as practicing Freemasons proud of our organization and of what it achieves and proud to propose a worthy neighbor or friend for friendship. . . .

Let me conclude with this parting thought from Shakespeare's *Julius Caesar:*

"Men at some times are masters of their fates; The fault, dear Brutus, is not in our stars, But in ourselves, that we are underlings."

I agree with Cassius. In the final analysis, our future will be what we make it.

During 1984 The Philalethes *published this six part series on leadership. It was well received and the editor of this publication felt it should be a part of this "Search for Leadership" and retained in a permanent form.*

1. Working With The Principles Of Leadership

1. The Confused Executive

"Enthusiasm has to come from the top down. It can't come from the bottom up." This was a "teaser" in an article found in one of the dozens of magazines on computers I read each month. It's a truism in any project, not merely computers.

Far, far too often we find not genuine enthusiasm at the top in Freemasonry. We do find "leaders" giving lip-service to the need for leadership. But that's usually where it ends—on the lips. The necessary action is lacking.

"Management for a non-profit organization! You're crazy!" That was among the kindest phrases cast on me when I first suggested, several years ago, we must adopt the principles of management in the Craft.

A few, far too few, of our Masonic leaders have learned the hard way that I was correct. In Freemasonry we've got to use the principles advocated for profit-making managers. If we don't, within two generations this Order will go the way of many others—into oblivion.

You don't believe it? Do a little research. It doesn't have to be too time-consuming. Check and see what has happened to many fraternal organizations over the years. Look at what happens to far too many businesses. It is estimated (and I believe charitably) that 50% of new businesses are dissolved within two years. Within five, over two-thirds are gone from the scene. Why?

In almost every case you will find a lack of knowledgeable leadership along with under-capitalization. Look at both of these reasons objectively. Poor leadership; not enough money. Sound familiar? You can bet your tin cup it does. It does because it's exactly what has been, and is, occurring in Freemasonry.

Let's look at the money angle for a moment. Not all the appendant bodies are operating on a rotting limb. A few have been able to build up large bank accounts. They know how to get money off the top. Others are trying to be of service to the Craft by collecting pennies (actually) per member. But far, far too many of our Lodges and Grand Lodges are trying to operate in a 1984 economy on a 1954 monetary structure. That's a little difficult, even with magical powers.

Many years ago Dwight L. Smith warned against killing the goose that lays the golden egg. His warning hasn't been heeded. The Lodges and Grand Lodges are desperate while a few appendant bodies are salting away large sums. The goose is being rapidly suffocated. The time has come for this bird to look at the total picture. It's time for new designs to be drawn on the trestle board.

Perhaps it's the lack of money that has created our confused Masonic executives. There hasn't been enough money to educate them properly— Masonically, Search the budgets of almost any Grand Lodge, or Grand Body, to try to find a sufficient sum set aside for Masonic education. You'll search in vain. These bodies may have "education committees." If they do they have but little cash of the realm to work with.

This leads to Masonic educators who know little more than those they're trying to teach. A man is appointed to go forth into his district, or jurisdiction, and create Masonic disciples. He isn't told what to teach or how to teach. He is given no prior training. Fortunately a few rise above the confused executive. They learn by trial and error. They teach themselves. They have to. They are never given any tools to work with.

"Very few managers are sending their employees to computer training," claimed another teaser in the computer magazine article. Amazing! Even profit-making organizations are ignoring the facts of life as the "non-profit" associations do. The new computer operators are being forced to do what the Masonic educator has been doing for centuries—learn on their own. There are evidently confused managers out there as there are confused leaders within the Craft.

What can be done to whip this confusion? Not much—if we continue to sit on our dubious laurels of the past. Not much—if we continue to allocate pennies for Masonic education but thousands to keep the ritual "pure." Nothing—if we expect to cure the ills of centuries overnight.

Almost fifteen years ago I was invited to meet with an Education Committee of a Grand Lodge. It was concerned. Members were suspended every year in large numbers. There was no continuity among the officers of the Grand Lodge from year to year. Few were attending the state-wide educational conferences. Education was at a low ebb. The Committee wanted to know what could be done to turn the tide around.

Having spent fourteen frustrating years on a Grand Lodge Committee on Education I could speak with a little authority. At that time I had produced two training films based on my book *Key To Freemasonry's Growth*. Among other things, I suggested they place a copy of that book in every Lodge; that

The Confused Executive has all the tools of the modern electronic age to work with. He doesn't know what to do with them, and probably considers them intruments of the devil.

they start using the films (one a year) along with the film's *Leader's Guide*; and that they hold a state-wide "Wardens' Workshop" immediately after the close of the Annual Communication of the Grand Lodge. BUT, this should be done only if they could be certain of a five year commitment.

All the Grand Lodge officers were present that day. They discussed the proposal at length, then agreed to start and continue the program for five years. They did a tremendous job. The tide was reversed. The fruits of that commitment are still apparent.

A Grand Master, over the strong objections of many in his Grand Lodge, agreed with his Director of Education and permitted four two-day seminars to be conducted during his year. These were based on *Key* using the five training films. The participation was excellent. Although not many Masons were reached, those who were present have worked wonders in their areas of influence.

In both of these cases we did have "enthusiasm from the top." This is rare, as we all know. So, perhaps we should take another look. Perhaps we should try building enthusiasm from the bottom!

It's easy to say "It Can't Be Done!" Then we don't have to do anything. But I've been heartened by the results from some of those Master Masons who were once at the bottom. Some reached the top and did tremendous jobs against continuing opposition. Others are on their way to the top and are dedicated to the principles of the need to know more about Freemasonry. They won't be "confused leaders."

What can we do to take confusion out of the Craft? Try to put more enthusiasm into the leadership. If we aren't successful, start at the bottom. It will eventually reach the top. Let's give those service organizations working for the *Craft* dollars instead of pennies. Initiate, or support, efforts to spend more money to educate our members. Keep in mind—*there is nothing more expensive than ignorance.*

Don't get discouraged. Learn all you can about Freemasonry. There's plenty of help available from several sources. Become a teacher, then teach. Remember that what you learn isn't worth much unless you share it with others. Ideas locked in your mind are worthless until you put them to use.

2. Building Leadership

The leadership of any progressive organization realizes new leaders must be constantly developed. I prefer to use the term "grown." Why? Because contrary to the thinking of many, leaders aren't born—they are developed, or grown.

Let's be honest, though. The leadership of many organizations, and these include Lodges and Grand Lodges, don't really want to develop leaders. They don't want anyone to come along who will "out-shine" them. Proof? How often have you heard a former presiding officer say: "We didn't do that in my year. We're not going to do it now." "I'm against raising the dues. I didn't have any extra money to spend when I was the Master." I've heard these, and many other such statements within the past month. And the list can go on indefinitely.

Then we must ask: Does the leadership have the patience and perseverance to train new leaders? Do we really want to spend the money necessary to develop the leaders of tomorrow?

There are two types of leaders in every organization. Douglas McGregor considers them "Theory X" and "Theory Y" managers, or leaders. "X" believes workers must be coerced and controlled; "Y" feels workers want to work and are capable of self-motivation.

I agree with his thinking, so I call these leaders—*Obstructive* and *Constructive,* because this is more descriptive for us non-managerial types. It should be readily apparent that the *Obstructive* leader will accomplish little, or nothing, in a voluntary organization such as Freemasonry. Unhappily, we have far, far too many of this type throughout the Fraternity.

Constructive leaders are needed if Freemasonry is to prosper. They will put the welfare of the Craft above their own egos. They will surround them-

46

selves with "strong" men and help them in every way to be better than previous administrations. They recognize the world is changing. Differing skills must be used to build the organization. We must train men who are willing to take the time and spend the money necessary to grow the leaders of tomorrow.

Space is short, and I believe we all can easily recognize the Obstructionists who surround us, so we'll concentrate on putting Constructive leadership to work.

We quickly learn in management that we *get things done through other people.* To accomplish anything that's important, we must learn to work with others. To do this we must have a working knowledge of the principles of management. I know it is claimed management and leadership aren't necessarily the same thing. True. But try being a leader without being somewhat of a manager!

There are thousands of management consultants. All have differing ideas. They must have to survive. But most (never all) do agree there are certain principles a Constructive manager must follow. These are:

PLANNING * GOAL SETTING * ORGANIZING * STAFFING * COMMUNICATING * CONTROLLING.

We'll cover each of these at some length in future articles. For now I'll summarize them for our purpose of building leadership in Freemasonry.

PLANNING allows us to accomplish the GOALS we set. Goals must be set realistically. They should not be overly difficult to achieve, nor should they be too simple. They should be established by ALL who will be required to reach them. Your goals may mean nothing to me, but if I help you set them they become mine, also. You can bet your tin whistle I'm going to do everything in my power to reach the goals I set!

Planning is also important in ORGANIZING, STAFFING, COMMUNICATING, and CONTROLLING. Actually, there's no way one can be a leader without knowing how to plan. These are necessary for building leadership. And, frankly, we have a greater nucleus of leaders in Freemasonry than you will find in *any other* organization. We have never used them within the Craft as we should. We have been ignoring them and many potential leaders. Why?

Because they have characteristics we've been warned against. They may look too much like "trouble-makers." They're aggressive because they want to do a top-notch job. They seek perfection, but realize they'll never reach it. Here are some other things to look for in the potential leader:

He Desires criticism; Seeks responsibility; Has ideas and is creative; Solves problems; Works toward goals; Initiates action; Is independent; Adjusts to reality.

If this doesn't sound like the type of man you want on your team, see if this explanation will convince you.

Constructive criticism, not praise, gives him the evaluation of what he has done. He's tough on himself. He's continuing to try to improve.

He needs responsibility. He wants jobs that have a certain amount of risk (not physical) to them. He wants to be creative; to work toward goals he has helped set. The tougher the job the better.

Solving knotty problems is fun to him, not work. He wants to put the pieces together. He realizes no one man knows all the answers, so he will seek advice with these problems. Then he wants to be left alone to complete the job. He's not a "book and rule" person. He develops short and long range goals for himself. He'll help his superiors plan their goals, if they will let him. These goals will be kept flexible so they can be adjusted to reality.

Notice the word "fun." That's the key! If we enjoy what we do, if we have fun in doing it, we'll contribute to the success of any organization.

FUN! That's what we've got to have in Freemasonry. My late friend Conrad Hahn put it this way: "Masons should radiate the joy of wisdom." This joy and fun in Freemasonry can come in a countless number of ways.

Festivity was what helped build the Grand Lodge system of Freemasonry in the early 1700's. Exposés frightened the leadership in England. The "fun" was taken out of Masonry. This helped bring about the formation of the "Antients" in 1751. The festive board once again became an important part of the meetings. The reunion of 1813 once again took away the festivity and brought back "formality."

The festive board brought "fun" into Freemasonry in the early days in America. Then all types of organizations "for the betterment of man" sprang up. For varying reasons Masonry went along with much of their preaching. The festive board was abolished. It must be revived if the Craft is to reach its full potential. It will come back with Constructive leadership.

What does a Constructive leader look like? It's hard to say. He'll come in many shapes and sizes. But you can be certain the Constructive leader will always: *Give recognition*; *Encourage creativity*; *Request assistance*; *Accept blame*; *Give credit*; *Seek advice*; *Practice participation*.

The forefathers of today's Freemasons knew that man must have recognition. (This will be developed at length later.) We're supposed to recognize this even now, aren't we? Don't we hear the Senior Warden tell us he's charged to "Pay the Craft their wages, if any be due." How often this is ignored! Men who have more than earned their "penny" are allowed to leave the Lodge without receiving a pat on the back.

I've said this several times since I put it into the script for my first full length leadership film: "Industry and schools too often use the lord-serf, or cattle baron approach to education. The belief that one man knows everything, a *few* know a little, but the masses know nothing, is almost as prevalent today as it was a hundred years ago. This is the obstructive approach to education. It prevents growth; it represses creativity."

Every day I find this statement strengthened, even in this "enlightened" age. Yet, this approach never has and never will work in Freemasonry. Often the members know more than the leaders. This causes boredom to set in. It causes the Lodges and Grand Lodges to disintegrate.

The type of men we have in Freemasonry won't be driven. The Constructive leader knows this. So he *requests* their help, then leaves them alone to get the job done. He gives them credit for their accomplishment. If anything goes wrong, he takes the blame. Then he'll try to determine why it went wrong so it won't happen again.

Only the obstuctionist doesn't seek advice. The world is too complex for anyone to be an expert in everything. This brings about participation. With participation anything can be accomplished, without it success is dubious.

The year before I became Grand Chancellor of the Grand College of Rites I learned a Board had decided the College would be disbanded the year after I served as Grand Chancellor. When I took office I informed the members I had no intention of presiding over a dying organization. There were many untapped avenues the Fellows in the College could follow. Several were outlined. The Fellows of the College were asked to help. They did. We had an excellent year. The College has continued to grow. The man I had the pleasure of starting in line five years ago, Jerry Marsengill, will preside over a prosperous and growing Masonic organization.

It's easy to quit. Too many have given up. This is why we must have Constructive leadership—now. We must start looking for the leaders of tomorrow. We must build the future leadership by using what Constructive leadership is available today.

Freemasonry's problem? It's not the lack of leadership as we often hear. We have an abundance of leaders. We are not using them in Masonry. We're driving them into other organizations where they feel they can serve a useful purpose. Where they can put their creativity to work.

A man uses less than 20% of his creative ability in his avocation. That's what the experts say. I believe its lower. But at least 80% of this creative force is wasted. What an asset this would be in Freemasonry—if we would put it to work!

Let's do it. Let's put Constructive leadership to work. Let's build our Masonic leadership.

3. The Necessity For Planning

"You've made a believer out of me," said a Grand Lodge officer at the conclusion of a planning session. "I never would have believed a random group of men could accomplish more than an individual."

We had held a four hour session on planning and goal setting. I had outlined the steps necessary for planning. We had discussed these steps freely. I then passed out a NASA test and we took a trip to "the moon" alone. The participants then counted off. Those with like numbers became a TEAM. No chairman or leader was appointed. Each team went into another room. There they discussed each point on how to return safely to the mother ship from their crashed vehicle.

When the short allotted time was up the teams returned. The lowest and highest individual scores were posted. The scores for each team followed.

Without fail each team score was better than any individual score.

This "test" has been used many times. The results are always the same. They prove that a group of men of reasonable intelligence, any group even picked at random, can accomplish more than can any single individual. This is encouraging, except to the egotist.

We discussed the steps in planning some more. The participants became different groups charged to set a goal and formulate the plans to reach the goal. Many confessed later it was the first time in their lives they had ever considered planning for anything.

Why should we learn how to plan? This can be answered by asking other questions. Why does one Lodge grow and another stand still? Why does one Lodge have an overflow attendance and another have to plead to have enough present to confer a degree? You have the answer. The successful Lodges have officers that set goals and make plans to meet them.

Here I'm using the word "Lodge," but what I'm saying isn't limited to Lodges. It goes for Grand Lodges, appendant bodies, commercial enterprises, and any organization.

IF IT WEREN'T FOR THIS BLINDFOLD....

The successful Lodge must continue to plan or lose its members to complacency. The unsuccessful Lodge must start planning or it will become defunct. But happily it can pull itself out of the rut. All it has to do is find someone who knows how to plan, then follow the plans.

This isn't as difficult as it may seem. Earlier I said there are excellent leaders all around us, but we aren't using them. Along comes the Grand Master of Masons in Indiana to prove I'm right. In the February, 1984, edition of *The Indiana Freemason* he wrote:

"If there is one thing I have realized as Grand Master that I did not fully appreciate before, it is the fact that a great many Master Masons in Indiana are ready, willing and able to help the Grand Lodge and their own individual Lodges.

"It might be that the very Master Mason who has never taken an active part in any Lodge activity just might be a most available worker for your Lodge if only he is asked."

He told a story about a Lodge that was ready to surrender its charter or merge with another Lodge. Along came a Master who turned things around. He found many Masons more than willing to help. He put constructive leadership to work. And you can bet your coffee mug it wasn't done without constructive planning.

The Master, and those he chose to work with him had to take a hard, cold look at what had happened and was happening. So, the Lodge was probably turned around because the Master found constructive leaders who could:

- Define the problems. These may have been poor ritual; poor programs; poor communication; little or no Masonic education; little or no knowledge of Masonic history, philosophy, or symbolism; no Masonic activity; little or no community recognition.
- Determine what training was required to alleviate the problems. These might be weekly ritual classes; a team to provide good MASONIC programs; a good editor for the bulletin; teams to teach the fundamentals of Freemasonry; a public and internal relations team to teach the members and public about Freemasonry.
- Determine the training objectives, such as excellent degree and floor work; improved attendance; providing the membership with information about all phases of Freemasonry.
- Determine the content of training programs.
- Decide what methods and techniques to use.
- Determine the supplies, materials and equipment needed.
- Decide when, where, and how the training will be done.
- Set aside the necessary funds to accomplish the objectives.

These are necessary steps in planning. There are times when more steps will be needed; at other times not as many will be required. You can add to them as you feel necessary. And you can elaborate on what should be done for your Lodge.

Without setting goals there is no need to plan. We must know what we want to achieve or there will be nowhere to go.

At the beginning of a management seminar I attended, the instructor told us to break into groups. That's all he said. We didn't know what to do. We had complete freedom, and it wasn't long before we realized that freedom without direction produces chaos. We spend several frustrating hours doing nothing. But we learned they weren't wasted hours. We learned that we had been wasting valuable time all our lives because we hadn't set goals early.

We also learned that goals, if they are to be intelligible, must be set through participation. All involved in trying to reach a goal must be allowed to add his ten cents worth. A goal set by me becomes my goal. You *may* help me reach it. But if you help me set that goal, it belongs to both of us. You are also committed to try to achieve it.

Please reread the above paragraph. If you remember nothing else, remember that. Many worthwhile goals are lost because that simple principle isn't followed. Put another way: PARTICIPATION ACHIEVES GOALS! It's the only way they will be reached.

Long ago I stopped asking for a vote on just about anything. A majority is one more than 50%. In setting and achieving goals you'll get nowhere with a percentage like that. Work toward a consensus. By give and take you'll find your team will meet this consensus and all will be committed to achieve the goal or goals. This requires learning to listen, an important but usually ignored principle of constructive leadership.

I've said this before, and probably will many more times: "The fellow who says he's too old to learn new things probably always was!" The same phrase fits the man who claim's he's too old to try new things. Don't put them on your goal setting teams.

Once the goal is set, what do we do? Follow the steps outlined earlier, but add these where necessary:

- Determine the purpose for the existence of Freemasonry
- Determine the responsibility of the Lodge to the Grand Lodge (or vice versa)
- Gather information
- Analyze the factors involved
- Form assumptions about the goal and plans
- Determine the budget required
- Set a timetable for reaching the goal
- Identify the role of the leader
- Identify the role of the members
- Define the needs of the members
- Determine the Lodge's role in the community
- Follow a plan of action
- Set standards and performance measurements
- Take corrective action where necessary
- Continually review, reconcile and modify the plans

Follow these steps in your planning process and see what a difference it will make.

4. Communication

"I can't get anyone to come to Lodge," is the all too prevalent cry. "We had an excellent speaker. He traveled over 200 miles to get here, but only 21 men showed up to hear him," one Master lamented. These and hundreds of other anguished statements are heard constantly.

Why? Why can't we get more than five or ten percent of our members to come to our Lodges? Why won't the members, and visitors, come to hear an excellent speaker? Perhaps, just perhaps, it's because of a lack of communication. We don't get the message out.

During a workshop I conducted I mentioned that our Lodges were wasting money by printing and mailing their "trestleboards," "bulletins," or whatever you choose to call them. The reason? Of the 50 or so that cross my desk each month about one percent are worth looking at. The others are filled with the names of officers, past masters, committees, and members. A short space is left for the Master, or Secretary, to tell the members there's going to be a meeting. Why the meeting, other than to fulfill the law, isn't mentioned.

The wrath of a goodly number of those present fell upon me. One Master, indignantly, told me he kept his messages short, because "my members are busy and don't have time to read!" Another goodly number backed up my statement and chided that Master (who hasn't spoken to me since). Not too surprisingly, many of the bulletins improved over the next several months.

You can bring in the greatest Masonic speaker in the world, the best out-of-state degree team, or have other excellent programs and have no increase in attendance. Or you can reverse the trend. It's communication, or the lack of it, that will make the difference.

Do you know that Freemasons should be good communicators? Isn't rhetoric one of the liberal arts and science we should master? It says so in our ritual, and our ritual is "supreme." Ask almost any ritualist if this isn't true. Then ask the ritualist what the ritual means. You just may be amazed.

Aristotle discussed rhetoric, or communication, at length. In it, he said, we must search for "all available means of persuasion." This Third Century B.C. Greek philosopher wrote his books on Rhetoric more for lawyers than the layman. Yet, his system for communicating hasn't been improved on over the centuries. Thousands of volumes have been written on the subject, but those worth reading espouse the principles of Aristotle.

I'll digress for a moment to note a parallel in my statement with that of Freemasonry. Over the centuries there have been millions of words written and spoken about morality and brotherhood. None have improved on the true concept taught, but seldom learned, in the Craft. That old axion about the more things change the more they stay the same holds true.

"Rhetoric," wrote Aristotle, "may be defined as the faulty of observing in any given case the available means of persuasion. This is not a function of any other art." He later added: "Of the modes of persuasion furnished by the spoken word there are three kinds. The first kind depends on the personal character of the speaker; the second on putting the audience into a certain frame of mind; the third on the proof, or apparent proof, provided by the words of the speech itself." How can anyone improve on this?

The man who is to be believed must be able "(1) to reason logically, (2) to understand human character . . .and (3) to understand the emotions." And can we refute his claim that "of the three elements in speech-making—speaker, subject, and person addressed—it is the last one, the hearer, that determines the speech's end and object."

Aristotle's advice to speakers is just as important for writers; they are communicators, also. He emphasizes that to communicate "one must study three points: first, the means of producing persuasion; second, the style, or language, to be used; third, the proper arrangement of the various parts of the speech" (or communication).

Let's set up a model to follow, based on Aristotle's logic of the Third Century B.C. and what communications experts of today follow:

1. the communication source;
2. the encoder;
3. the message;
4. the channel;
5. the decoder;
6. the communication receiver.

These are the main ingredients, although there are many other aspects to consider. But what does this jargon mean? Let's take a simple example:

You meet a friend in a coffee shop. He expresses a desire to become a Mason. You believe he'll make a good one, so you decide to discuss Free-masonry with him. You become the COMMUNICATION SOURCE. You construct a message through your nervous system. Your speech mechanism serves as the ENCODER; it produces the MESSAGE about the background of Masonry. This message is transmitted by sound waves thereby becoming the CHANNEL. Your friend's hearing mechanism picks up your message and becomes the DECODER for the COMMUNICATION RECEIVER—your friend. If your message has followed the suggestions by Aristotle, the receiver will ask for a petition.

What you and I are doing right now follows the outline above. I'm serving as the SOURCE; my computer has served as the ENCODER (along with the printing press); the MESSAGE is contained on these pages; it's transmitted (CHANNELED) to you by way of this magazine through light waves; your eyes DECODE the words; and your central nervous system becomes the RECEIVER.

With a little thought this model can be put to work for every conceivable function. Even so, communication continues to be the weakest link in almost every organization. Because of a breakdown in communication the top doesn't know what the bottom is doing, and the bottom could care less about what the top thinks.

A breakdown in communication is one reason the Master who had an excellent speaker had no attendance. He didn't let the members know who was going to be in his Lodge, what they could expect, why and when they should be there.

Guide 13 is reproduced below from my book *Key To Freemasonry's Growth*. You will note the "source" (or sender) must be closely attuned to the "receiver" socially and intellectually for communication to be successful. This is true in oral and written communication. Although there are only 26 letters in our alphabet, they are formed into more words with more meanings than anyone can ever learn. The 500 most commonly used words have over 14,000 dictionary meanings! Can we wonder why effective communication is so difficult everywhere?

GUIDE 13

THE INGREDIENTS IN COMMUNICATION

S ⟶	M ⟶	C ⟶	R
SOURCE	MESSAGE	CHANNEL	RECEIVER
(Person or Group)	(Purpose)	(Method)	(Listener/Reader)
Communication Skills	Elements	Seeing	Communication Skills
Attitudes	Content	Hearing	Attitudes
Knowledge	Treatment	Feeling	Knowledge
Social System	Structure	Smelling	Social System
Culture	Code	Tasting	Culture

IMPORTANT — The SOURCE and the RECEIVER must be close to the same social level or there cannot be good communication.

To add to the difficulty we have "jargon"—language peculiar to an organization, profession, or occupation—and non-verbal expressions which can often convey a better message than voice or print.

Every member of every Lodge, every Lodge of every Grand Lodge has a right to know what has been done and what is going to happen. This can be accomplished only through communication. The day will come in Freemasonry, as it already has in many areas of business, when closed circuit television, or video cassettes, will be widely used. But, as Freemasonry is always years behind technical advances we have only the printed word with which to communicate. We must use it wisely.

Lodge bulletins and newsletters, Grand Lodge magazines and newspapers, should be well-written, thought-provoking, and full of Masonic news and inspiration. If this attempt is made by all concerned, there will be a whale of a decline in demits. Members quickly lose interest in organizations that don't keep in touch. Surveys have proven this over and over again. Yet, we continue to ignore this fact.

These periodicals must be written so they'll be understood. Bureaucratic writing should be avoided. Take this case: A plumber found hydrochloric acid was good for cleaning pipes. He told the Bureau of Standards this. The Bureau responded: "The efficacy of hydrochloric acid is indisputable, but the corrosive residue is incompatible with metallic permanence." The plumber thanked the Bureau for agreeing with him!

Another letter was sent by the Bureau: "We cannot assume responsibility for the production of toxic and noxious residue with hydrochloric acid and suggest that you use an alternative procedure." Again the plumber thanked the Bureau for agreeing with him.

The Bureau finally broke down and wrote: "Don't use hydrochloric acid, it eats hell out of the pipes."

Reminds me of when the problems I had in registering "Imagination Unlimited!" For months I received documents I couldn't interpret. But a phone call to D.C. always straightened me out quickly. After the fourth or fifth such communication I asked the fellow on the other end of the phone why he hadn't put in writing what he said over the phone. "We have forms we must follow," said he. "We can't treat you any differently than we do anyone else."

I agree. We should all be treated alike. We all should be given stuff we can read and *understand*. Whether the communications comes from Washington, lawyers, insurance companies, banks, or Freemasonry, we should be able to enjoy and understand what we receive. Isn't that what our *Guide 13* said? We must learn to empathize—to put ourselves in the other fellow's shoes.

Thousands of volumes have been written on the subject of communication. Thousands more will be written. We've only scratched the surface. But if you will follow what has been written, you'll find we've made a deep scratch.

5. The Difference Is People

Setting Up An Organization

"Two years ago I was a terrible Worshipful Master," said Ed Perkins, who was about to become a District Deputy Grand Master. "I've been ashamed of myself ever since. Now I want to do something about it, but I don't know how to get started."

Ed was talking to Conrad Hahn, the late Executive Secretary of The Masonic Service Association, the Senior Warden of his Lodge, and me. It was the beginning of the film *People Make the Difference*.

Among other things we suggested we review the principles of management some of which we've been talking about in this series. We can't do much organizing if we don't have an understanding of Goal setting, Planning,

Communicating, Staffing, and Controlling. The first three we've covered briefly.

It's important to remember that Freemasonry is in *the People Business*. This means we must continually take into account human nature. We have found that most of the barriers to success are included in this all-inclusive human nature. We've also found this same attribute produces what success we achieve.

All of us have prejudices that have been built in over the years. Much that we have learned has come from our environment, our associates, family and schools. Our education has been shaped by factors over which we had no control. We all look at life through restricted windows.

This is the reason I've found groups working better than individuals toward the achievement of common goals. When we remember that *meanings are in people, not in words,* this reasoning takes on more importance. A good example is the plumber mentioned in the previous article. You can find many other examples every day.

When we establish an organizational plan, these and many other facts must be taken into account. People *are not the same.* Every one of us *is different.* By using these differences, by putting the square pegs in the square holes, we'll build an organization of which we can be proud.

Organizing is another planning function. Perhaps this is why too many organizations, governmental agencies, businesses, associations, and not just Masonry ignore this important tool. People don't know what their duties are. They don't know what responsibilities they have. Too often they don't even know to whom they should report. Everyone's responsibility becomes no one's. Square pegs are being hammered into round holes. It won't work.

An example are committees. Every lodge and organization has them. Most of these are chaired by a man selected by the presiding officer. Too often these chairmen and his members are reappointed year after year—even if they haven't functioned adequately during the years before. It's the easiest thing for a presiding officer to do.

Isn't it time to remove the blindfolds? Isn't it time we evaluated what we're doing and not doing? Isn't it time to eliminate committees and establish *teams?* Then put men of differing knowledge and temperaments on these teams to work for the benefit of our organization.

Before we become too critical about what has, or hasn't, been done in the past we should do some re-evaluating. Have the duties we expect our committees to do been outlined? Have they been given specific tasks to achieve? Have they been asked to sit in on a planning session? Have they been asked to participate in setting goals? If not, let's put the blame where it belongs—with the leadership.

Let's select the best men we can find as chairmen of our teams. (If this word turns you off, use "Commissions.") Then let the chairmen select their own members. Those selected should not be "yes men," but they should be compatible. They should have differing backgrounds to make the teams well-rounded. Each member should be a potential leader. (For a description of leaders see the second part of this series.)

But teams will do us little good if we don't follow a plan for organizing the organization. So, let's look at five major steps we must take. These are involved with DUTIES, RESPONSIBILITIES, AUTHORITY, RELATIONSHIPS, and PERSONAL REQUIREMENTS.

We must determine what work or activities we want carried out. This must be determined by the total organizational plans for a specific period. This will lead to assigning specific duties to a specific team, or individual, or special group. Fulfilling these duties becomes the responsibility of those selected to reach the predetermined goals. Remember—these goals must be set by the participants after the final plan has been determined.

Participation is all important. The most successful Lodges are those where one man doesn't run the show; where the ideas of everyone are considered. With this type of atmosphere each man takes his responsibility seriously.

Responsibility without authority leads to complete confusion. Authority must be clearly defined. People must know to whom they are to report. They must be able to answer questions positively. They must know what they can and cannot do. And there's a difference between power and authority. Through power, commands will be obeyed, usually because of fear. No Masonic body can be successfully organized through fear. We must constantly remember our members don't have to do anything they don't want to do. They can readily tell the leadership where to go.

Although the Master is responsible for everything that happens in his Lodge, he will delegate as much authority as possible. No able man is going to accept responsibility without authority. When this authority is clearly defined the relationship between the officers, teams, individuals, Grand Lodge, and the Master will be harmonious.

It is claimed the hands of Freemasons are tied because of Grand Lodge laws. This is not true. There must be laws, rules and regulations to follow or there would be complete chaos. But the laws found in Freemasonry tie the hands of no right thinking man. The excuses we hear are from lazy leaders, those who use regulations as a crutch to do nothing.

Constructive leaders know that we must INNOVATE and CREATE or we are going to stagnate. We can be innovative and creative within the framework of Freemasonry. We can finally bring Masonry into the Twentieth Century without disturbing the landmarks and customs of the Craft. But it's going to take education and dedication to do it.

When we take personal requirements into account we'll look for these men who can be creative, innovative, and are potential leaders. We'll avoid those who continually say "yes" to the boss simply because he's the boss. He's the type of fellow who will agree with the bigwig that he should remain in left field when he should be playing second base. He'll let him stay in hot water.

No one man knows the answers to everything—unless he's an egotist. Each man has his own area of expertise. It's difficult to make a writer out of an expert carpenter. A plumber won't make a good brain surgeon. Don't let friendship, or popularity, force you to put round pegs in square slots.

If we're going to organize our Lodges and Masonic bodies for success we must put Masonically educated and dedicated men on our teams. We must practice participation. We must give these men the responsibility and authority to carry out their missions. We must find potential leaders, men who aren't afraid to say "No" when it's necessary. We must select as many teams as necessary to make the organization successful.

To help us do this, follow Guide 7, "The Performance Cycle," from my book *Key To Freemasonry's Growth* in setting up the organization and in every planning step. Set a *General Objective*; determine its *Purpose*; set *Primary Goals*; develop *Strategies* which are sub-goals; *Check the Progress* periodically; *Review* and take appropriate action. But don't overlook these other important steps in *Organizing: Duties, Responsibilities, Authority, Relationships, and Personal Requirements.*

GUIDE 7

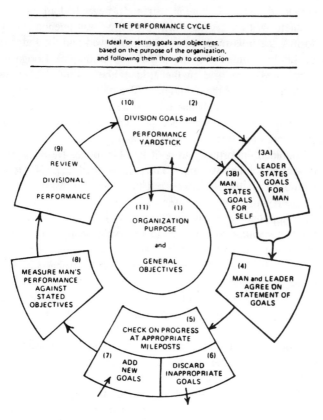

From *Key to Freemasonry's Growth,* Macoy Publishing & Masonic
Supply Co., Richmond, Va.; Copyright 1969.
Used by special permission.

59

Management, or leadership, is as old as man itself. "Scientific management" came in with the beginning of the Twentieth Century. After eighty-
four years isn't it time to incorporate it into Freemasonry?

6. Control *Is* Important

We can set crucial goals. We can adopt first rate plans to reach these goals.
We can even use that illusive ingredient called communication better than
anyone else. But if we don't control what takes place each step of the way, we
will have nothing.

Several have requested we set a goal of increased attendance and determine
the plans to reach this objective. So, let me tell you the story of what one
lodge did. We'll call it "Boondock Lodge" for want of a better name (and to
not advertise the one involved).

Boondock Lodge was to celebrate its 150th anniversary in six months.
How it had survived this long no one knew. Since the memory of man it had
needed the help of visitors to confer degrees. It never had a program for any
meeting. If there was no degree work, the lodge was opened, but never in
"ancient form," the bills read, the minutes approved and the lodge closed.

It can be safely claimed that the officers of Boondock Lodge had been
collecting treasures—treasures in the attic of their minds. They were not
about to throw away any of the old cliches. The old ways of doing things were
too valuable to be discarded. It had taken time, money and effort to acquire
them. Why do away with them and accept new-fangled ways of doing things?

A young upstart was elected Master for Boondock's 150th anniversary. He
saw this as a golden opportunity to revitalize his lodge. He decided to focus
this rebirth around the anniversary. To do it he needed help. Not too surprisingly he found this help. He discovered there were a few members of his
lodge who had been looking for some leadership.

The Master appointed committees (Teams would have been much better) to
find an excellent speaker, to plan a banquet, to clean up the building, and to
advertise the event. He and his officers brought in a ritualist to teach them
how to open and close the lodge. He didn't want to be embarrassed before all
the visitors he expected.

The goal was set: a massive anniversary celebration with at least 200 in
attendance. The plans to reach this goal were resolved. The banquet committee would plan the meal and arrange for at least two sittings (the dining room
could hold about 100). The publicity committee would advertise the event far
and wide. The cleanup committee would scrub and paint. The officers would
learn the ritual.

The committees did their job. The night of the big event arrived. One
hundred ninety-eight Masons were present to hear a prominent Past Grand
Master speak. At 10:45 p.m. the Master introduced him!

"My Brethren," said the Past Grand Master, "I drove almost 200 miles to
be here this evening. I've spent over sixty hours working on my speech. Now

I'm too tired to give it and you're too tired to listen. I'll just say you've had a glorious 150 years. I hope the next 150 will be just as glorious. Good night."

What went wrong? The committees evidently did their jobs. The goal was reached. The plans to attract a large attendance worked. Almost 200 showed up in a lodge that normally had ten or less in attendance. The officers opened the lodge with a letter perfect rendition of the ritual. The meal was appetizing. Why the catastrophe?

There was no control. There was no central authority coordinating every step of the way. The Master had made certain the ritual would be perfect. He forgot there is much more to running a lodge than the ritual. He had appointed committees but failed to check what they were doing. Each committee worked without knowing what the others were doing. There were no joint meetings of these important workers.

The time set for the banquet didn't allow enough time for two sittings and still start the meeting at the appointed hour. Two hundred men was the goal set. There wasn't enough food for 150. The stewards had to run to the local chicken food restaurant for boxed dinners for the balance. This delayed the meeting even more and got the evening off to a poor start.

The Master rapped his gavel more than an hour late. After he had opened the lodge he went through the whole gambit—reading minutes of previous meetings, reading and balloting on petitions, introducing every visitor regardless of his rank, and even insisting each "say a few words." Some, as always, had more than a few words to say.

Not many men have the courage of that Past Grand Master. Most will take much abuse and still try to make the leadership look good. Or, perhaps, they are in love with the sound of their voice and will speak every chance they get and under any circumstances.

Again let's look at the principles of leadership. We must first establish goals or we'll merely go around in circles accomplishing nothing. BUT all goals *must be chosen by the people involved.* Always remember, your goals may not be important to others. Goals set through the participation of those involved become their goals, also.

Then there must be plans developed to reach the goals. Control factors must be fixed immediately. With control comes measuring factors. Goals and plans can never remain static. As we move toward the achievement of the goals, plans, and even the goals themselves, may have to be modified. Everyone involved must be kept fully informed and up-to-date about needed changes. The coordinator (controller) will make certain they are.

You can plan the best program in the world, but if no one knows about it they won't be participating. Intelligible communication is again important. This should follow the formula reporters have been using for years: what, when, why, and who. It's better to tell 'em more than they need to know than not enough. The facts must be accurate. Communication must be controlled.

The Teams (or committees, ugh!) should have the best men available. It's always good to have men of varying experience on these Teams. They will compliment each other. You should organize and staff your small groups for the benefit of the lodge as a whole.

Long ago I stopped asking for a vote on any subject. I found a majority is one more than 50%. A majority decision can prove disastrous. It's much, much better to get a consensus, so work at it until a consensus is achieved. Then you can't go wrong.

Most important: control, coordinate, measure the results each step of the way. Don't leave anything to chance. Assign responsibilities and authority. Remember that everyone's responsibility becomes no one's. Don't assume—know.

Passing this short series along to you has been good for me. It has made me think. I have been getting in a rut because much of my work is done by me alone. But I had to stop "preaching" and put some of these "words of wisdom" into practice recently. I find they still work. I find they do take the hassle out of leadership. I hope you will find they will do the same for you.

As with all things, an end must be reached. It is claimed we never complete a story or an article—we have to abandon it. This is the case here. The tales of lousy leadership could go on forever. The possible solutions can be demonstrated even longer. If I have caused you to consider this major subject, my job has been a success. If you start reading books and articles on leadership and management, my reward will surpass all expectations.

Good luck. Good leadership.

This was a talk presented to the Masters and Wardens Association of Richmond, Virginia, in 1968. It became the basis for the opening portion of Key to Freemasonry's Growth *which was published the following year.*

Masonic Leadership

"Have you ever seen a Worshipful Master who knew the ritual any better?" asked a visiting out-of-state Mason of his friend as they left the Lodge. "He did such a beautiful job, I sat back after the opening knowing I was in for a pleasant evening. But was I in for a surprise! After the flag was saluted he was tongue-tied, nervous, and at a complete loss about what to do next. Without his secretary we'd still be meeting. Why? What type of Freemasonry do you fellows have in Virginia? You must teach the ritual perfectly, but you evidently teach nothing else."

"Unfortunately, you are correct," said his friend. "We have schools of ritualistic instruction run by the Grand Lodge Committee on Work every year where an officer of a Lodge can take his family for a vacation while he learns the ritual—and he must learn the ritual before he is eligible for nomination for Worshipful Master, then, too, most of our Lodges have weekly classes in the ritual. But with few exceptions, nothing is taught about Masonic Law, protocol, custom, or leadership. It is amazing, when you stop to think about it, why some of our Masters do as well as they do.

"There is a ray of hope, though," continued his friend. "For over ten years our Grand Lodge Committee on Masonic Information, Research and Publications has been plugging away at the void in our Masonic Education. Some of its members spend long, tiring hours working for the Craft. Each year Area Conferences on Masonic Education are held in ten different localities and members of the Committee lose time from their regular employment to travel to these meetings; they spend sleepless nights considering our needs; they bring to us information about Freemasonry that they have gathered from long years of experience and from the school of "hard-knocks." Hopefully, we will someday devote almost as much time to Masonic Education as we now do to Ritualistic Education."

All of you know this is not an imaginary conversation. All of you have heard Worshipful Masters praised and condemned based on the manner in which they presided during a Communication. (In short time you are going to learn what a Worshipful Master is supposed to be, so we will dwell on that, but) let us discuss Leadership for a few moments.

A Masonic leader is a peculiar character. In many respects he must be the same as the leader in industry, politics, schools, civic clubs, or any organization that requires strong administrators. But the Masonic leader must differ in at least two respects: First, he must be an acceptable ritualist—he should not expect those under him to do what he cannot do; Second, in no organization does the presiding officer have the power, or the responsibility, as that of a Worshipful Master. In every other organization the body controls the presiding officer—in Freemasonry the opposite is true. . . .No one, not even the Grand Master, can tell the Master how to run his Lodge as long as he complies with the Constitutions of Masonry, the Laws of the Grand Lodge of Virginia, and the by-laws of his Lodge. As long as he does that, he can operate his Lodge as he thinks best. Consider the power he has; then consider the responsibility that must go with it!

A good leader is one who can get the best that is in them out of those who are under him. A good manager will realize he cannot do everything himself and that he does not know all the answers. But a good leader will know where to turn to get things done and for the answers he needs. And he will give credit to those who deserve the credit, thereby earning the loyalty and respect of everyone.

In Freemasonry loyalty and respect are as necessary as in industry—perhaps more so. The worker is paid a salary or wages in industry—in Freemasonry what the members do is done gratuitously; loyalty and respect cannot be purchased, they must be earned. And how does the Masonic leader earn them?

He must make the members who work with him feel what they are doing is important—and it is! In a play the fellow who has the smallest part is just as important as the actor who gets the headlines. If it is not done properly, the whole play will be a disaster. In the Degree work, the Junior Deacon and Seafaring Man are as important as the Master. The solemnity of the work will be destroyed if anyone doesn't do what he is supposed to do at the proper time and with respectful decorum.

The Worshipful Master must let every member know he is interested in him. If a member misses a Communication, the Master should contact him as soon as possible to find out why. Let him know he was missed, that his presence is important to the Lodge, that what he does for the Lodge is appreciated.

The good leader, Masonic and otherwise, will find men he can depend on to get a job done—then give them the power and authority to do it. This will not only give the leader the opportunity to think, plan, and ease the pressures placed upon him, but will develop better leadership for the future. The leader will be providing goals and expediting better teamwork; he will find the quality of the performances will be greatly improved.

There are some Masters who will not delegate authority and will not give credit to their members because they are afraid they will not get the praise due them; or because they have an unclear idea of the responsibility that rests upon the shoulders of a Master; or because they do not know how to delegate authority or work. They do not realize they are weakening their own position and the Lodge when they let their fear rule their minds and actions.

The good Masonic leader will be receptive to the ideas of his officers and members. He will listen to all proposals and all sides of any suggestion. He will consider the pros and cons and after determining if it is good for his Lodge and Freemasonry, will adopt or reject the proposals or suggestion. He should be objective in his thinking and not let personalities influence his decision. He must remember he is Worshipful Master of his Lodge and not any particular faction.

There is no quick, cheap, and easy way to master the art of leadership. But the Mason who has intelligence, aptitude, and is interested in the philosophy and teachings of the Craft, can learn the principles and techniques of leadership and apply them. And there is plenty of room for Masonic leaders. Three hundred and forty-three Worshipful Masters must be elected each year in Virginia, which of necessity means there must be 343 Secretaries and the same number of Treasurers. When you add 1,372 line officers to this list, you have some idea of the magnitude of the statesmenship necessary in Virginia Freemasonry on the local level. But this does not tell the full story, for every well-governed Lodge must have several working committees if it is to be at all successful. This means at least 9,000 more Masons must be put to work for the Subordinate Lodges. When we add another 2,000 Masons to serve as Grand Lodge officers and committeemen, we find the necessity for leadership is acute and unending. More and more of those coming into the Craft will demand better leadership—or they will stay at home, go into some appendant body, or drop out of Freemasonry entirely. The day has been gone for many years when the intelligent Mason will accept and honor lackadaisical leadership.

How many times have you heard Past Masters say, "I'm now a 'has-been' and not wanted?" But how wrong they are! If they have learned the teachings of Freemasonry and really want to work for the Craft, there are jobs to be done. There are many fields in Masonry going begging for the proper leaders: History, Ritual, Education, Writing, Editing, you name it, it's there.

Because a Mason is elected to the high and honorable officer of Worshipful Master does not insure his success as a leader, but it is an opportunity to prove that he is one. He must not stand heavily on his title; he must earn the respect his office deserves. He must remember that he owes it to those who preceded him and those who will follow to uphold the dignity and authority that goes with the title of Worshipful Master. He must remember it is not Joe McGillicutty presiding in the East but the Worshipful Master of blank Lodge. And how does he uphold that dignity?

First: By having an acceptable knowledge of the Ritual of Freemasonry as taught by the Grand Lodge Committee on Work.

Second: By having a thorough knowledge of the Methodical Digest.

Third: By having studied the Officers Manual.

Fourth: By putting into practice the Mentors Manual.

Fifth: By choosing qualified and dedicated members of his Lodge to head up and work on the many committees necessary to the well-being of all Lodges.

Sixth: By being Master of the whole Lodge and not any one faction.

Seventh: By training his officers in the fundamentals of Freemasonry so that they can surpass him when they assume the leadership of the Lodge.

Eighth: By keeping his members informed of what the Lodge has done and is planning to do.

Ninth: By informing his members of the glorious history of the Craft and by providing intelligent programs on Masonry.

Tenth: By following all the foregoing and more.

In summary: Leadership—good leadership—is the key to the success of Freemasonry throughout the free world. The Masonic leader must be willing to sacrifice his time and money for the benefit of the Craft, and expect nothing in return. He must be a servant of all, forgetting his personal pleasure and convenience. He will have to overlook the jeers of the cynics and shirkers and those who are critical of all who truly work. There will be no monetary reward, but the Master's Wages earned will be without comparison. To be "worthy of respect" should be the goal of every Master Mason.

"Growing the Leader" is a term I've been using for years. I like the term, because I don't believe leaders are born—they're developed—or grown. Most have to "grow" themselves into leaders. Yet, there's no such thing as a "self-made" man. All of us must depend on others for our knowledge. It comes from teachers in our schools, books we've read, conversations we've taken part in, motion pictures we've seen, discussions in churches and organizations, and in dozens of other ways.

What follows appeared just before Conrad Hahn died. He had this comment: "It seems, Friend Allen, as if you have 'dumped the whole load' on this subject; hope you've saved some 'leadership training' material." I have—bushels of it!

Growing the Leader

"A survey of the Lodges in any given area will provide what Dr. Elton Mayo discovered in the Hawthorne Study," I wrote in **Key to Freemasonry's Growth.** "The amount of production is not governed by management standards, but by work-group standards! It was not basic intelligence, dexterity, or latent ability that determined productivity. It was the relationship of the individual to the group with which he worked.

"This indicates that the Grand Lodge can set all the standards and measurements it wants to. It will accomplish little or nothing if the principles (standards) of the Lodges are not in agreement. The average member is going to reflect the qualities, or lack of them, of the Lodge he joins."

The Hawthorne Study referred to was made over a 16 year period. It made an "amazing" discovery—workers produced more if their hours were shortened—and more if their hours were lengthened! Unbelievable? That's what almost everyone thought. That's one reason this became one of the longest studies of management and workers ever attempted.

What was the unknown factor causing workers to produce regardless of the physical conditions? It was something not too deeply hidden in each of us—
Recognition! "By making the worker a part of the team; by asking for advice and cooperation; by making each person feel important, each felt that he was a major factor of the whole, his work took on purpose; he acquired a necessary sense of responsibility; he was no longer a cog in a machine."

These statements were made by me in 1969 in the same book, and today, eight years later, I would underline every one of them. I have seen them proved over and over again. For the purposes of Freemasonry the "worker" is changed to "member" and the Lodge grows or disintegrates according to the type of leadership.

There are basically two types of leaders—**Constructive** or **Obstructive.** I say "basically" because it may be truthfully argued that there is a type somewhere between. Here we'll discuss the Constructive and Obstructive leaders.

The **Obstructive Leader** believes people must be coerced into accomplishing anything; that people must be controlled constantly or they will achieve nothing. He tells his subordinates what he expects of them and directs their every action. He assumes no one wants to work, so the worker must be threatened and driven. Ambition and responsibility are things only he seeks.

Obstructive leadership works fairly well in industry. There the worker is paid to put in a certain number of hours and to perform certain tasks. It won't work in Freemasonry, or any voluntary organization. The member isn't a "worker." He can tell the leader exactly where to go. Usually, though he says nothing. He merely stops attending meetings.

On the other hand, the **Constructive Leader** gives few, if any, commands. He recognizes the ability of his subordinates. Together they discuss and reason out the goals **they** want to reach. They become a TEAM, **not a committee.** If the Team is successful, the leader gives the individuals the credit; if the Team fails, the leader takes the blame.

There is a definition of a committee that I like: **A committee is a group of men who individually can do nothing, but who can, collectively, decide that nothing can be done.** Think about that for a moment. When was the last time a committee that you are familiar with accomplished anything? If it did, who did it? One man—the chairman?

The committee system is so deeply imbedded in the American way of life people have difficulty believing committees accomplish nothing. You really have to look no further than the Congress of the United States to note how futile committees are. Even so, in my leadership seminars I have to graphically prove this point. We appoint committees with chairmen and give them a task to perform. It doesn't get done. Then we let individuals try. More gets accomplished. But when **Teams** selected at random tackle the task, it's amazing what they achieve.

Teams are constructive; committees obstructive. Teams work by consensus; committees work under one-man rule. Quite frankly, I will not serve on a committee anymore. As an individual, yes. As a member of a Team, yes.

The beliefs and traits of the **Constructive** and **Objective Leaders** are graphically compared in Guide 2 in **Key to Freemasonry's Growth.** Guide 3 in the same book shows how to recognize the potential leader.

The **Constructive Leader** will grow leaders; the **Obstructive Leader** retards or destroys the potential leaders who surround him. Unfortunately the obstructionist doesn't recognize his faults. Talking to him is the same as preaching in church. You reach the people you can count on.

The potential leader of any organization is goal-oriented. He seeks feedback and wants his performances evaluated. He looks for personal responsibility and an opportunity to be creative. He has a high drive and wants goals with a certain amount of risk to them. Problems for him are fun to solve. He is more than willing to initiate action. Above all, he can readily adjust to reality. His counterpart is just the opposite.

In the Masonic Service Association Audio Leadership Course I emphasize the word "fun." This is the key to the success of every Lodge, or organization, profit and non-profit. A world-renowned manager put it this way: "Business is fun. Companies that generate excitement about what they are doing are more successful than those that don't." So are Lodges.

A young lady, 15 and pregnant, and in trouble with the law, was asked to define the qualities of a leader. She wrote: "To me a leader is many things. He is strong, but not by force. Leaders usually know how to make decisions. They know where the real fun is. A leader helps to make one's mind wonder what to do next. One who leads is usually ahead of the rest. He knows when and where to expect trouble. He may be experienced, bull-headed and even smart. To me, that's what a leader is. To most he's considered to be brutal, sometimes violent and quick."

This young lady hadn't been exposed to management seminars or behavioral scientists. Yet, she has described many of the qualities brought out by the trainers of leaders. She does add one thing, though, that few teachers ever mention. She has the "key" to being a successful leader that others overlook—FUN. As she said, a leader "knows where the real fun is."

FUN! That's what we've got to have in Freemasonry—fun, yet with dignity. "Masons should radiate the joy of wisdom," is the way Conrad Hahn phases it. FUN! That's why I've emphasized the use of **Teams.** Teamwork is fun. It's sharing of experience and knowledge. It helps men to grow into leaders.

Our "ancient Brethren" designed Masonry to be fun. In those Lodges where this concept is followed there is growth because there is fellowship. Best of all, they are growing into leaders.

According to many psychologists, industry and schools too often use the lord-serf, or cattle baron approach to education. This is the belief that one man knows everything, a few know little, but the masses know nothing. It's almost as prevalent today as it was a hundred years ago. This obstructive approach prevents growth; it represses creativity.

This relationship, where the baron tells his foreman what he wants done and the foreman forces his men to do it, will no longer succeed. It never has in Freemasonry. Frequently the workers know more than the boss; the student, the professor; the member, the officer. Boredom will set in. The system, or the Lodge, disintegrates, or at best, stagnates.

Lodges are going to grow—forward or backward. Obstructive leadership will drive them back. Constructive leadership will carry them forward. The individual Freemason will determine which way his Lodge is going to move.

Published in The Philalethes, *this is not exactly a "tongue-in-cheek" article. It's a plea to place a major need for Freemasonry at the top of the agendas of our Grand Lodges.*

HERESY?!

PROFESSIONAL FREEMASON NEEDED. Successful candidate must be knowledgeable about Masonic law for this jurisdiction, must have a reasonable concept of the ritual; must be Masonically well-read; must be a diplomat and able to get along with the leadership, must be able to teach Masonic subjects and develop leaders. A Mason who is self-taught is preferred as he will be expected to establish the criteria for teaching. Should be a Past Master or one who has held a higher position. Has to be willing to travel constantly throughout this jurisdiction and stay in the field for days at a time. Will be expected to work every weekend and 80 to 120 hours a week, 52 weeks a year. Must have own transportation for which he will be reimbursed at 10 cents per mile, one way. The per diem while in the field will not exceed $10 per day. The salary will be commensurate with his years of experience as a Mason and manager, but will not exceed $3,000 per annum. Take advantage of this opportunity to be of service to the Craft.

This article was going to be titled "Do We Need Professional Masons?" It was changed because it shouldn't be a question, it must be a fact. We absolutely do need "Professional" Masons. We need them to turn members into *Master Masons*.

The mythical help wanted advertisement was not written wholly with "my tongue in my cheek." Of course, the "professional Mason" has an evil connotation in many quarters. No Mason is expected to reap any coin of the realm for his service for the Craft. He is expected to share his knowledge, acquired over the years, often at great expense. He should readily agree to travel hundreds of miles to deliver a 20 to 30 minute address, which he has spent days preparing, without being reimbursed even for his out-of-pocket expenses. Forget an honorarium!

71

Not too long ago I traveled several hundred miles to speak at an assembly. While there I was present when several officers complained because $100 was paid to a non-Mason who was one of the speakers. It was pointed out that dozens of Masons would have been happy to do it for nothing. The complainers didn't consider that no one else could have made the same presentation as did the fellow who traveled a couple of hundred miles to be there.

There have been, and still are, many men serving on Grand Lodge committees and never reimbursed for any expenses, not even travel and lodging. On a personal note, for over thirty years I've written books for and about Freemasonry. For over fifteen years I've produced motion pictures for and about Freemasonry. There are many who sneeringly term me a "professional Mason." Ah! I've netted from my books and films over that whole period less than a Grand Secretary makes in one year. Thank goodness I'm a professional manager in the business world or my family would have starved years ago.

Many of the most respected and admired Freemasons were, and are, "professional Masons." An example is Harry Carr of England who recently died. If you think on this subject for a few moments you can name at least a dozen more. Yet, we should thank God for them. Imagine where our Craft would be today without them.

Someday, I hope, we'll be reading advertisements for Professional Freemasons. They are needed, desperately needed. But they must be paid a living wage so they can devote full time to working for the Craft. It's impossible for any man to give the time necessary to the needs of Freemasonry if they must make a living in another field. Contrary to what most believe, it takes time, money, experience and hard work to develop programs that are practicable. It can't be done piece meal. It can't be done on a part-time basis.

Too often we forget the workers in Freemasonry are volunteers. Unlike the workers in the "outer-world" they don't have to do anything for the Craft. Thousands never do. But I've always believed, and still do, that hundreds among those thousands would gladly serve under the right conditions.

What are the right conditions? Take another look at the advertisement. That's a glaring statement of the wrong conditions. Our volunteers are expected to give up their weekends throughout the year to serve. If their expenses are reimbursed it's close to the ridiculous figures noted. Too often they are "self-taught" mainly because there are few who know how to teach them.

During the question period after I had stopped talking at an assembly last summer, Harold Elliott, II, MPS, suggested we stop rushing men through the "degree mill." The reasoning behind this was to teach them the "basics" of Masonry. I asked this PGM from New Jersey who would do the teaching while they were waiting. With his usual wit he said: "I don't know, but there's you and me."

The right condition for the making of Master Masons is to provide enlightened leadership. This is recognized far and wide except in Freemasonry. We're constantly hearing the cry to develop leadership. But for the most part that's all it is, a cry. We're not putting our words into action. Why? Is it because the leadership doesn't want leaders? Is it because we don't want the *status quo* to change?

Within the lecture I gave at the first Assembly and Feast for The Phila-lethes Society I claimed the ritualists have always controlled the Craft. The leadership of the Fraternity has almost without exception come from these ritualists. I claimed they are not about to give up their control by developing leaders outside their ranks. I have seen nothing since then to change my opinion. If anything, I've seen my opinion bolstered.

Those familiar with the "Peter Principle" know that all of us finally reach our level of incompetency. A good salesman doesn't necessarily make a good sales manager. An adequate attorney doesn't always make a good politician or judge. An outstanding engineer seldom makes a good administrative offi-cer. So it is with an excellent ritualist. Most of them make horrible adminis-trators.

So, what's the answer? To get back to the "basics" we hear so much about but rarely see. These basics are found in Anderson's *Constitutions*. These *Constitutions* are outlined in *Key To Freemasonry's Growth:* "Officers must be chosen by merit, not by seniority or favoritism. . . .Masons must do hon-est work; Masters must pay just wages; envy of a Brother is forbidden; supplanting a Brother in his work is not allowed; Wardens must be true to the Master and Brothers must obey them; young Brothers shall be instructed to continue practicing Brotherly Love; Grand Lodge must approve working tools."

Doesn't this give us the basics of Freemasonry? Doesn't every Grand Lodge still adhere to the *Constitutions* as outlined by Dr. James Anderson as printed in 1723? Shouldn't we learn and follow these *Constitutions?*

If we'll stop giving lip service to the *Constitutions,* the tenets and precepts of Freemasonry and put our words into action the Craft will rebound. We'll develop the leaders we must have. We'll find the "professional" Masons we need to lead us triumphantly into the Twenty-First Century.

During World War II Freemasonry throughout the world grew tremendously, in the free world, that is. In countries controlled by Germany, Russia, and other dictatorial governments, Masonry was abolished, or almost so. In the United States the growth was stupendous. Throughout the history of the Craft we find growth whenever there's a war. We aren't always as careful as we should be about who we take in the West Gate.

In peace time we pay the price. Many men don't find what they are looking for in Masonry. They don't because in the rush to keep the degree mills grinding we take no time to explain anything about the Craft. Members begin to quit in large numbers. Or they let themselves be suspended for non-payment of dues. Lodges find themselves in trouble, financially and numerically. The organization begins to break up.

During recent years we've heard much lamenting about the decline in membership. Yet, much of it is the fault of the leadership. Many of those who leave would gladly remain IF they could find something in our Lodges other than ritual.

What follows will give you a brief sampling of why organizations fall apart.

The Breakdown of
An Organization

We've often heard and read about the "Fall of the Roman Empire." This has become a newsworthy topic in recent years. Seldom do we hear about the breakdown of organizations. Even when we do we rarely consider the reasons they disintegrated.

Nations, empires, organizations (including Masonic Lodges and other fraternal bodies) usually don't fall apart because of outside forces. The "enemies" are found within their structures. These enemies causing the breakdown include:

- Poor leadership
- Inefficient communication
- No understanding of the purpose for existence
- Bureaucratic control
- Loss of membership
- Confusion
- Collapse

The scenerio goes like this: Poor leadership brings about inefficient communication. This causes the purpose for the organization's existence to be poorly defined, it it's defined at all. This enables bureaucrats (people never elected to office and accountable only to their own kind) to gain control and then consider self before others. A loss of membership is the result, and this brings about financial problems because the income structure is deflated. Confusion is so wide-spread the collapse of the organization follows.

Unfortunately we don't note the symptoms until the loss of membership is so pronounced it is no longer a whisper. In many cases the "enemy" has infiltrated so deeply the organization is lost. And lost it will be if there is Obstructive leadership at the top when the shout is heard. This type will rant and rave, waving its arms frantically, accomplishing nothing. An unhappy ending is inevitable.

Constructive leaders, on the other hand, will sit down quietly with those who have a wide range of knowledge. They won't be "yes-men." That's one thing not needed at this (or any) stage. They will be men who can constructively view the whole picture to determine what went wrong. Then they will work out goals to reverse the destructive trend and devise plans to reach those goals.

The first step is to put Constructive leadership to work. This will call for leaders who will surround themselves with men who know more than the top does—men who have varying degrees of skill—men who are acknowledged experts in their field. For some reason the Obstructive leader won't do this. He must show he knows more than his subordinates. Consequently he curries only to incompetents. He doesn't realize incompetency breeds more incompetency, and this brings into being bureaucracy.

One of the goals must be to strengthen communication from the top to the bottom. Effective communication is acknowledged to be the weakest link in every organization. Without question it is difficult to pass along the intelligence needed for success to every person in the chain of command. It must be done if the organization is going to grow rather than stagnate or disintegrate.

Unless the purpose for existence is clearly defined, and through effective communication passed along to the membership, the organization is doomed to failure. Without a purpose, no organization can long exist. It will be controlled by self-seekers—men who will use it to their advantage. They will be concerned only with what they can get out of it. Obstructive, or incompetent leadership will permit the few to control the whole. But the whole won't let this go on indefinitely.

Once the membership really realizes a few incompetents are "running the show" they are going to say, "Enough!" They will quit the organization. The exodus starts in dribbles then expands to a flood. And the organization will die if enough members quit. The financial coffers will dry up thereby curtailing necessary programs. Then the "bureaucrats"—the self-seekers—will desert to look for greener fields. The resulting confusion will bring about the organization's collapse.

A grim picture, isn't it? It is, but only if we will let it happen. It can be prevented by putting our trust into the constructive people every organization has in abundance.

You'll note I've said Communication is the weakest link in any organization. It is. But why is really a mystery. Hundreds of volumes have been written on the subject. Some of them have been excellent. Several schools of instruction on management have produced motion pictures on the subject (including Imagination Unlimited!). Seminars are being held throughout the country almost daily. Yet, communication is still poor.

Freemasonry is notorious for the lack of communication. Conferences are held in just about every section of the country yearly. Some excellent papers are presented. Outstanding ideas are brought out—unfortunately these are rarely developed. The papers are usually buried. The Craft seldom has an opportunity to see or hear anything about what goes on during these conferences. The Conferences of Grand Masters and Grand Secretaries is no exception. Yet, the Craft pays the expenses of these delegates.

The article that follows barely touches on the subject of communication. I hope it will strike a responsive chord and you'll search a little deeper.

Communication

WHAT IS IT?

It's the weakest link in any organization. That's what communication is. You've heard that statement, if you've been listening. If you haven't been listening you're contributing to the problem. Because one of the reasons for poor communication is poor listening.

Listening, a part of communication? That's strange, isn't it? Isn't communication passing on information from one person or group to another person or group? It is. So how does listening come into the picture?

The fellow passing on information is called "the sender"; the one getting the message is called "the receiver."The next time you are the "sender" watch the "receiver." He'll be giving you "feedback" by his attitude. If he's gazing into space, he isn't listening. If he's not listening, his feedback is telling you that you aren't getting anywhere. You aren't communicating, even though you're talking.

Listening is one of the most difficult, if not the most difficult, of the communicating skills. It's also the most neglected. Yet, it must be learned through continual practice if we're to become real communicators.

Learn to "listen" with your eyes as well as with your ears. Your eyes will "hear" much that your ears will miss. MEANINGS ARE IN PEOPLE, NOT IN WORDS. Meanings are frequently conveyed by actions rather than in words. Watch the actions and bearing of the receiver. The feedback will prove invaluable.

Whenever I give a speech (or call it what you will), I watch the audience. Each member of this group sends me a message, even though I'm doing the talking. Words from them aren't necessary for me to catch their feedback. If they're paying attention, or appear to, the chances are that my message is getting across. If many of them are coughing, squirming, or looking anywhere but at me, I cut my talk short. I'm not particularly fond of hearing myself rave. Unless the audience is with me I may as well go home.

Whose fault is it when the receiver doesn't listen? It's not his. It's the sender's. When you have something worth passing on, make certain the receiver gets the message. Ask the receiver questions on the subject. Make the subject a cooperative, participative, effort. Also, make certain the message you want to convey is worth listening to.

"We communicate to change, or affect, human behavior," said Conrad Hahn in the leadership film *Breaking Barriers to Communication*. Also brought out in the film is a statement by David K. Berlo, a Professor of Communication Arts: "our basic purpose in communication is to become an affecting agent, to affect others, our physical environment, and ourselves; to become a determining agent; to have a vote in how things are. In short, *we communicate to influence—to affect with intent.*"

Human behavior! Something new to think about in communicating? No, it certainly isn't. Aristotle, who was born in 384 B.C., in talking about communication effectively claimed a person must be able to understand human character and behavior in their various forms; he must reason logically; he must understand emotions. So, the Human Behavioral Scientists aren't as modern as we may have thought.

A few of the barriers to effective communication we must "listen" for include: human nature; organizational realities; assumptions; prejudice; fear; low trust. As each of these is related to human behavior, we must remember those of us in Freemasonry are in the "people business."

The "people business" is the toughest to be in. But it need not be, and it won't be if we'll learn to listen. This is what Thomas Edison did. He claimed he wasn't really a great inventor. Most of what he invented was based on the ideas of others. All he did was listen to their ideas. Then he developed them.

Non-verbal communication can be as important as verbal, and more so at times. Benjamin Franklin is an example. No one could use sound and the printed word more effectively than he. Yet he realized there were times when it was more effective to act and say nothing. That's how the streets of Philadelphia were lighted. He could see the value of well-lighted neighborhoods, but he knew the city fathers would howl about the expense. So he set up a lantern outside his home. People carefully feeling their way home in the dark came to the well-lighted area around his home. They saw the value of his action. It wasn't long before his neighbors placed lights about their homes.

He had achieved his goal. He had overcome organizational realities by using non-verbal communication. His neighbors had "listened" and followed his example.

Listening—it's merely one phase of the important art of communication, but it's certainly all-important.

A few years ago Imagination Unlimited! developed a motion picture entitled "Breaking Barriers To Communication." *We were fortunate in having the inimitable Conrad Hahn discuss the subject. It has been popular with some governmental agencies and in industry, although it's designed for the leadership of Freemasonry.*

Here's a condensed version which will help you, if you put the suggestions into practice, break the barriers to communication.

Can We Break the Barriers to Communication?

Before almost every seminar I conduct, I project a cartoon with a man jumping up and down. He's saying, "I don't want to hear it. It can't be done!"

And the fellow's right. If he doesn't want to hear it, it can't be done. If we won't listen, we'll accomplish nothing. If we believe it can't be done, then by golly, it can't be done.

This is one of the most important keys to breaking the barriers to communication—listening. Sounds strange, doesn't it, when we say listening is an essential ingredient in communication? But there are only two ways I know of to learn. One is through listening; the other is by reading. Then to improve on what we've learned, we must do it.

In every organization, in every business, in every profession, everywhere, the lack of effective communication is the weakest link to success. Without it, the bottom doesn't know what the top expects. And those on the bottom could probably care less. But unless the top knows what the bottom is thinking, there can be no growth.

Assuming (which you'll find is always dangerous!) your Lodge wants to grow, let's look at a few of the barriers to good communication:

- Human nature
- Organizational realities
- Assumptions
- Prejudice
- Fear
- Low trust

81

To be perfectly technical, each of the barriers is related to the first—human nature. So, let's remember Freemasons are in "the people business."

Let's also remember why we want to communicate. David K. Berlo, a professor of Communications Art, gives this definition: "Our basic purpose in communication is to become an affecting agent, to affect others, our physical environment, and ourselves; to become a determining agent; to have a vote in how things are. **In short, we communicate to influence—to affect with intent."**

"To make it even shorter," said Conrad Hahn in **Breaking Barriers to Communication,** a Leadership Training film, "we communicate to change, or affect, human behavior. There is really no other reason for communicating."

It's interesting to note these modern day communicators haven't improved on the thinking of Aristotle who was born in 384 B.C. He claimed for a person to communicate effectively he must be able to understand human nature, character, and behavior in their various forms; he must reason logically; he must understand emotions.

Let's look at **organizational realities** as a barrier. A volume could be written on this subject. Not having that much space, I'll just touch upon the stifling of ideas, something too prevalent in too many organizations. This is usually caused by the fellow at the top believing he knows the answer to everything. He's not interested in the ideas of anyone—just his own.

Without ideas, freely expressed and freely discussed no organization can grow. This takes **teamwork,** not "committee-work," nor one-man-ship. It means organizations should have policies rather than iron-clad rules and regulations. With the latter, the worker/member won't feel free to be creative.

Assumptions cause us to make mistakes in judgement, because we assume our words and actions mean the same to everyone. We forget (if we've ever given it a thought) all of us look at life through restricted windows. Our vision is no broader than our environment, our associates, our work, our hobbies, our reading, our organizations.

If we'll take this into account we'll practice **Empathy.** Empathy is the art of putting ourselves in the other fellow's place. If we do that, we'll be able to communicate with anyone in a meaningful way. If we do that, we'll really be Constructive Leaders.

The film lists these methods of **Breaking the Barriers to Communications:**
- Discard the "Crutch"
- Talk about ideas
- Utilize non-verbal communication
- Use examples
- Danger—I assumed!
- Don't prejudge
- Learn to listen
- Welcome feedback

Organizational realities are used as a "crutch" by the Obstructive leader to do nothing. He can always find an excuse to be lazy in the rules and regulations of any organization, especially in Freemasonry. The Constructive Leader will use them as guides, not obstacles. He won't lean on a "crutch" of any kind. So, let's discard the crutch and communicate.

Ideas kept locked in our minds are useless. It is said that for every idea put into practice there have been at least ten people who thought about it. That's the trouble. Talk about your ideas. Work with them. You will be amazed at how often you'll see them worked out to completion.

Non-verbal communication is used constantly. A raised eyebrow, a handshake, a frown, a grin, a pat on the back all have a meaning to someone. Everyone knows what a mere wink can do. And non-verbal communication can speak volumes at times when words would do more harm than good.

Using examples can work wonders. For example: someone tells you a line is crooked. Perhaps it is, but if we place a straight-edge along side it, we'll know for certain. Will lighting a high-crime area keep down thefts? Put up more lights and find out. What makes one Lodge more successful in attracting attendance than another? Look for the reasons. Will they work in your Lodge? Try them.

"I assumed!" are two of the most dangerous words in real life. They are deadly to effective communication. We can't assume the other fellow has received our message until we make sure he has. We find out by asking questions. Remember this: MEANINGS ARE IN PEOPLE—NOT IN WORDS. The 500 most common words have over 15,000 dictionary meanings. So, never assume the other fellow puts the same interpretation on your words as you do. Then, too, we must not draw conclusions until **all** the facts are in. We must stop making snap judgments.

If we'll stop pre-judging, prejudice will disappear. Conditions are changing daily. Past experience or teachings may be completely different today than they were yesterday. Our thinking may be based on insufficient knowledge, and it may not fit present circumstances anyway. We should consider the other fellow's dreams, then we'll learn to appreciate him more. When we do, we'll be able to communicate on the same level.

Gossip contributes to every barrier to communication. Truth is the only way to stop gossip. As Truth is considered a "divine attribute" in Freemasonry, gossip should be unknown among the Craft.

Listening is all-important. We can't communicate if we can't listen. And we should learn to "listen" with our eyes as well as our ears. Meanings are often conveyed by actions rather than words. Frequently our eyes will "hear" more than our ears.

Feedback is part of listening. Feedback is information communicated upward, downward, and sideways—to our superiors, our subordinates, and our equals. Feedback is the only way to learn how well, or badly, we're doing. The Constructive Leader seeks feedback; the Obstructive Leader wants no part of it. Feedback, if there is any, tells us what kind of atmosphere we have in our organization. If there is no fear of superiors, if there is trust, if there

Meanings Are In People - NOT In Words

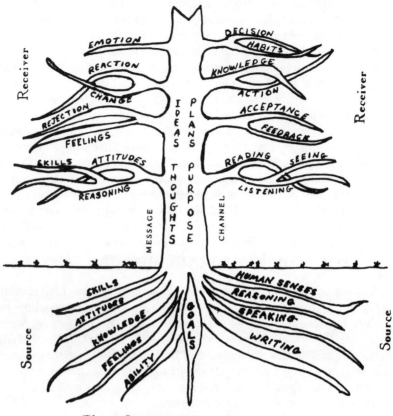

The Communication Tree

are good listeners, there is feedback that helps us grow.

In **Key to Freemasonry's Growth** there is a guide showing the five senses—seeing, hearing, feeling, smelling, and tasting—are the channels used in communicating. Most important, we find the Sender must be close to the same social level as the Receiver. Communication skills, attitudes, knowledge, their social system, and culture must match or effective communication can't occur. But, there are ways to overcome even this barrier in many cases.

If we remember—MEANINGS ARE IN PEOPLE—NOT IN WORDS—we can put ourselves on the other fellow's wave length.

It can't be done? Of course it can. By working at it, we can break the barriers to communication. If we do, then we'll grow.

Feedback is probably the most important tool in communicating. Far too often it's ignored. This will give you a start, but only a start, on the subject. What you do with it can make a whale of a difference in everything you try to accomplish.

Feedback: An Important Tool in Communicating

Communication has always been, and probably always will be, the weakest link in the building of any organization. I said that earlier, didn't I? Yep. I've been saying it for years, and expect to continue to say it for years to come.

Earlier we discussed the importance of listening as a tool in the art of communication. I also used the word "feedback" once. But it's a word that should be used over and over again any time we discuss communication. Why?

Feedback tells us what we need to know. Unfortunately for the timid, it doesn't always tell us what we'd like to hear. In fact, feedback is completely discouraged by the *obstructive* leader. He knows all the answers, so why bother him with what we may think?

The *constructive* leader seeks feedback. He wants to produce the best possible results. He knows no one man can possibly know all the answers, so he seeks the expertise of others. He'll accept all the feedback he can get, then weigh it. He won't throw an ounce away that can be used.

In seminars I conduct I often stress one item by saying: "Every man in this room knows something that no one else in this room knows." Eyebrows always go up at that statement, so I'll add after a moment: "Think about it, then tell me you disagree." Slowly the eyebrows come down. In every group there are many, many types of occupations represented. Even those who have the same basic occupation have knowledge that's different from others. I don't care where you go or what you do, you know something no one else knows. And everyone knows something you don't know.

So, don't you need the feedback from others? Isn't it worth cultivating? Sure it is. It can make you appear better than you really are. It has often worked for me. There's so much I'll never know it makes me shudder.

85

Thankfully, I usually know whom to call on for the feedback I need.

What is feedback? It's information communicated upward, downward, and sideways. It goes to and comes from our superiors, our subordinates and our equals. By listening carefully, we can determine how well or badly we're doing. By evaluating the feedback we receive we can improve what we've done, or are about to do. Constructive feedback will help us reach our goals.

That is, it will help us reach our goals if we really want to. There are some goals that are set, yet there are efforts to make certain they aren't reached. Sounds strange, doesn't it? But I'm certain you can think of many instances where this has proven true.

Have you ever heard some influential member of a Lodge or organization state how strongly he's for a plan under discussion? Have you heard him throw stumbling blocks in the way to make certain the plan won't be adopted? Here's an example: "I'm certainly in favor of air-conditioning this hall. It's true more members will be attracted to our meetings. BUT—the committee has come in here with a proposal that will bankrupt this Lodge. My own investigation proves the job can be done for one-fourth the committee's figures. Then, too, it will cost thousands to remodel this building to hold an air-conditioning unit. When you add the cost of insulation required, we're in trouble. This is a worthy cause. No question about it. It should be done. BUT I think another committee should be appointed to work on it. Better still, we should start putting money into savings now so that we can do the job right even if it takes a couple of years."

The feedback of those "BUT's" will do a job every time. They've killed many a worthy proposal. They've also destroyed the reputations of many men. We praise on one hand, then drive in the knife of the "but" with the other.

The speaker in the above example seldom attended his Lodge. He didn't want the Lodge air-conditioned. It might have caused his dues to be increased. He didn't care whether the attendance was good or bad. The comfort or discomfort of those attending Lodge meant nothing to him. He was present for one purpose: to kill the proposal. He fed the Lodge untrue statistics. He destroyed the morale of the members of the committee who had done an honest job. His feedback almost destroyed his Lodge.

A short time ago a Grand Secretary told me he was hearing from the officers of the subordinate lodges in his jurisdiction about Masonic education. He said the feedback he was getting indicated the educational program wasn't being graciously received. The fellows were getting tired of year after year hearing about how they should contribute to the Masonic Home. The need to improve the blood bank was stressed. The youth organizations came in for their share of time during every so-called educational workshop. So were other topics not even remotely connected with Masonic education.

He readily granted that each of these topics is worthy and should be discussed. A workshop, or seminar, on Masonic *education,* he was now convinced wasn't the place. The feedback he had received was working. If he can convince the education committee of the need to revise its long-standing format, the Freemasons in that jurisdiction will be the winners.

This is how feedback works. A committee is responsible for education. It presents this product to those who need it throughout the state. It controls the product. The fellows in the boondocks let the committee know what it thinks of its product through feedback. They don't have to buy it by attending boring workshops. If they stay away, their message becomes clear. Feedback has done another job.

The importance of feedback is often overlooked. As students, we can affect the teacher. If we don't understand something, if he's sensitive to feedback, he'll repeat it. If we're receptive to a speaker, he'll get the feedback and give us a better speech. Our feedback influences our friends and family. It does if we let them know they're doing a good job, or assist them in times of need.

Feedback is a reaction. We can, and should, become aware of this reaction and use it to help us grow.

Conrad Hahn commented on the Long "Welll": "A word gone to 'l!" This can be carried a little further. The Lodge, Grand Lodge, or organization that doesn't plan, is going to 'l. And far, far too many Lodges have never given a thought to planning.

After you've read the article, why not take a pencil and paper and make a list of what you've seen amiss in your Lodge, and others, during the past 12 months. Then if you're really ambitious, go back several years. You'll be amazed at what you'll find. With rare exceptions most Lodges have no goals. Perhaps that's good. If you've got no goals then you'll need no plans.

After you've read this brief account, again I hope you'll want to go into the subject much deeper. Try it. You'll really be glad you did.

Planning

"I'm concerned about the direction our Lodge is going," said the Junior Warden. "The attendance is declining every month. And we aren't doing anything constructive."

"Wellll! I don't know how you can say that! We had over three hundred in our Lodge only four months ago," countered the Worshipful Master.

"That's right. And we blew it."

"What do you mean 'we blew it'? That was the biggest attendance we've ever had. Fellows came from all over. There has never been anything like it in our District before."

The Junior Warden nodded. "I agree with that all right. It was a golden opportunity for Masonry and our Lodge. Most of those fellows hadn't been in a Lodge in ten years."

"So what are you squawking about? We got them there didn't we?"

"Yes, Sir," agreed the Junior Warden. "Your committees did a darn good job in advertising our 150th anniversary. And we got the best speaker in the State to help with our celebration. And you blew it."

"That's twice you've accused me of blowing it. Get specific. I haven't got time to listen to a lot of sour grapes." The Master was visibly upset.

"You started the meeting 35 minutes late and there was no excuse for it. You balloted on petitions when they could have been held over another month. You had the minutes read and let the secretary monopolize over a half hour. You had all the visitors introduce themselves, which I consider discourteous and even invited them to say a few words. It was after 11 o'clock when you got to our speaker—a prominent Past Grand Master.

"I'll never forget the words of that Past Grand Master when you finally called him to the East," the Junior Warden continued. " 'Brethren,' he said, 'I spent over 60 hours researching this speech. Now I'm too tired to give it, and you're too tired to listen. I'll just say that your Lodge had a glorious 150 years. I hope the next 150 will be just as glorious. Thanks for inviting me. Goodnight.' "

This is a portion of the opening scene of the motion picture **Planning Unlocks the Door.** It happens to be a true incident. It also happens to be something that occurs far too often in far too many Lodges. Why? Simply because of the lack of planning.

This article could be filled with episodes of poor planning that one man encountered during the last 30 years. You could add several more pages to the list. The important thing now is to try to correct these past errors. Now is the time to start planning properly.

Why don't we plan properly? It could be because we don't know how, but I suspect it's because planning is hard work. But the rewards should more than offset the work it takes.

Let's look at some reasons for planning:
- For change
- To build for the future
- For improvement
- To stimulate growth
- To increase efficiency
- To build morale
- To improve human relations
- To grow leaders

Now, you add at least another dozen reasons why proper planning is important. Take into account the planning we do today may well affect the lives of countless individuals for years to come. For instance: If the Worshipful Master we met earlier had planned his 150th anniversary properly, his members would have continued to attend his Lodge. They didn't. They were bored. They wanted no part of such slipshod proceedings.

Here are some steps to take to properly plan anything.
- Determine the purpose
- Set the goal (or goals)
- Gather information needed to reach the goal
- Analyze the factors involved
- Formulate assumptions
- Determine the budget
- Set a timetable
- Establish measurements
- Take corrective action where necessary

When we determine the purpose we must take into account Freemasonry exists mainly TO MAKE GOOD MEN BETTER. Let's say we want to do

PLANNING GUIDE

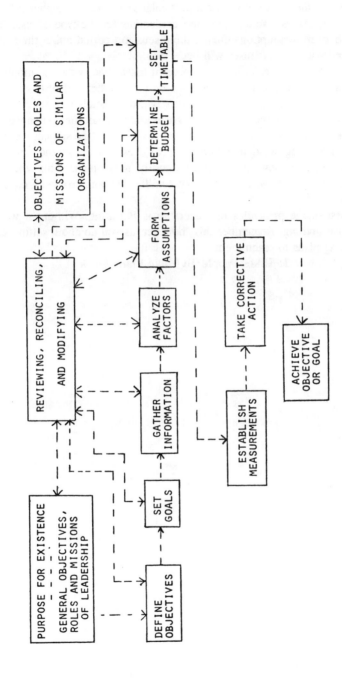

From the Leadership Training Film PLANNING UNLOCKS THE DOOR
Copyright 1972 by Macoy Publishing and Masonic Supply Company, Inc.
Copyright transferred to Imagination Unlimited!

this through Masonic education. This becomes our overall goal, or objective. To accomplish this objective for one of our Communications we want a good Masonic speaker. This becomes our particular goal. We then gather information about speakers. We analyze their credentials for the type of speech we want. We form assumptions during the discussion period about their availability and what the expenses will be.

And speaking of speakers, don't forget it takes time (which is money) to prepare a talk. It takes time to travel—even to the other end of town. Automobiles don't run on air. Meals cost money. So do hotels.

We must determine what funds we have available; determine when we want the speaker; and decide what measurements we'll use (the subject we'd like covered; how long we'd like him to speak). Now we take the corrective action needed by reviewing/reconciling/modifying our plans. This will determine who the speaker will be, the subject he'll cover, and how we'll cover his expenses.

The first of the principles of leadership is **Planning.** Without it we can accomplish nothing. Remember this, however, as you go about setting goals and making plans to reach them—

It Takes People To Make Plans Work

What was said about planning certainly holds true for organization. Where there is proper planning you'll find a well organized organizational chart.

I've often heard: "We don't need an organizational chart. The Grand Lodge tells us who's supposed to do what. The duties of the officers are clearly defined." Bunk! I don't know of any Grand Lodge that tells the officers what they are to do. Many offer suggestions. Many reward those Lodges that do what has been suggested. The basic duties of the Worshipful Master are established. But there's a tremendous gap in establishing an organization for any Lodge.

Too often we encounter officers who firmly believe the members know little or nothing. I call this the "cattle baron approach." That's where one man knows everything, a few know something, but the masses know nothing. And if you think this approach isn't valid in Freemasonry, do some more thinking.

If you study what follows, I believe you'll believe as I do—People Do Make the Difference.

Organizing the Organization

Study the cartoon accompanying this article. Then before you look any further down this page, think about what **you** see in it.

This is the title cartoon of the Leadership Training film by the same name— **People Make the Difference.** The film deals with organizing and staffing a Lodge, or any other organization. And it doesn't take long to discover there must be an organizational plan. Without one, men won't know what their responsibilities are because none are assigned. This is not only dangrous, it's disastrous.

When the participants in the seminars are asked what the lead cartoon means to them, the comments vary. Some are downright hilarious. Basically, though, they come to the conclusion that the characters are carrying their own weight. Through using a proper organizational plan, the staff has been placed in the proper slot. The "round pegs" are in the round holes; the "squares" in the square ones. This is an organization that's going to produce results.

To produce a plan for organizing it is necessary to follow the principles of leadership (or management). We've been discussing them over the past few chapters. We know what to look for in leaders and potential leaders: Those who seek responsibility; seek goals; prefer creative opportunities; likes to

make the difference

solve problems; initiate action; and adjust to realities. And the list can go on and on. But this will give you a starting point for selecting your staff.

Effective communication is indeed important. Internally we must be able to talk about ideas; use examples to get our points across; learn to listen to the other fellow; stop prejudging; and gladly accept feedback.

Externally communication is just as important. Every organization seeks, or should, a favorable public image. It doesn't take a lot of money to show Freemasonry as a force for good. It does, however, take men who know Masonry thoroughly. They must know how to tell the story truthfully. They must be able to counter the reporters who, mainly through ignorance, dislike the Order. They must know enough about Masonry to be able to answer any questions. In business "goodwill" is an asset. It is usually something earned, not purchased. No business can exist for long without it. Neither can Freemasonry.

Planning is something anyone planning to organize must be familiar with. Organizing is actually a planning function. In the last edition several reasons for planning were listed; so were some of the planning steps. Most of these must be followed in adopting an organizational plan for your Lodge.

Let's look at the five essential steps in organizing. They are:
- Determine duties
- Assign responsibilities
- Assign authority
- Determine relationships
- Determine personal requirements

Assuming (which is always dangerous, as has been pointed out) we know what the organization wants to accomplish, the leadership must determine the men needed. They've looked over the staff and know the capabilities of each person. The overall objective has been determined, but the means won't be until the men have been selected. Then **they** will determine how the objective will be reached. The duties will then be determined for the men assigned to the various tasks.

Along with duties must come responsibilities. Responsibilities not assigned become no one's. This usually means the job won't get done. Who can the leadership blame, or commend? Unless responsibilities are assigned, few, if any, goals will ever be reached.

Authority becomes a touchy subject. Only a Constructive Leader can share his authority without quaking. Yet responsibility without necessary authority isn't good. Few men worthy of getting a difficult job done will accept responsibility without the necessary authority.

The relationship among the Teams needed to reach the overall objective must be determined. What responsibility will each assume? When will each complete its assignment and pass it along to the next phase? Who will determine what? How does each affect the whole? What is the relationship of each to the Master, Grand Master, Lodge, community?

The personal relationship of each man must be considered. Each will have personal requirements to take into account. How much time can he take away from his other responsibilities—his job, his family, his church, his hobbies? Will these personal requirements prevent him from working with the others to achieve the overall objective by the predetermined time? If so, a replacement must be found.

When these steps have been covered you're well on the road to reaching the objective. You've placed the right men in the right slots. You should find the performance will be superior. Even so, remember Murphy's law: If anything can go wrong, it will. This is the reason good planning has a built-in rule: Check progress constantly, discard inappropriate goals, add new ones, measure performance, review, review, review.

There is one point that needs emphasizing. This concerns authority. Far, far too often this is not clearly defined. It must be or the organization is in trouble. Too often good men are given responsibility but not the authority to get the job done. It also determines whether or not a man is working **with** you or **for** you. And there's a whale of a difference.

It's easier, if you're lazy, to work **for** someone. Then you only have to do what you've told to do. You can sit back and wait for instructions. Then you won't be responsible for anything. If you work **with** someone, you'll be assuming the initiative constantly. You'll do your best to keep him out of trouble by advising him when you think he's going wrong. This means you won't be a "yes man."

Now, a word of caution. "Yes men" are usually popular. They seldom get in trouble. They get promoted more often than their counterparts. Of course, they often let their bosses get in trouble (you can find examples every day in the newspaper). They seldom complete a job, and rarely do they create anything. On the other hand, the fellow who isn't a "yes man" puts his job on the line constantly. Too often he won't get the chance to prove he's a good leader. The leadership fears he'll "rock the boat." Actually, he keeps the boat from rocking.

As you go about organizing and staffing you will find that **People Do Make the Difference.** No organization can be successful without people educated in its principles. They must know something of its ritual, history, symbolism, philosophy, and aspirations. They must be dedicated to its precepts.

You must follow the laws, rules, and regulations of your Grand Lodge. But these should be used as a ladder, not a crutch. You must be a Constructive Leader and constantly grow other leaders. You should work toward attaining the purpose for the existence of Freemasonry—**to make good men better.**

Several volumes have been written on Masonic jurisprudence, but nothing has been published recently. There is a great need for this subject to be examined. Mackey and Pound have been out-dated for years.

I've tried to point out a few of the differences between law and jurisprudence. There are many more. Too often our Grand Lodges turn to lawyers to write Masonic codes. And there is a vast difference between what goes on in a courtroom and what should go on in Freemasonry.

Lawyers aren't necessarily interested in justice. If this sounds harsh, think about it. Frequently you'll find the same attorney arguing both sides of a case, although not at the same time. There may be a lapse of months or years between the cases. They are interested in winning, period. Often if they don't win they don't get paid.

There is no room in Freemasonry for this kind of "justice." We don't need "civil law," per se in our Order. All Master Masons have taken an obligation to obey civil law and civil powers. If they don't they can be charged with unMasonic conduct and stand a Masonic trial.

There is a vast difference between civil *law and* Masonic *law, or as I prefer to call it, Masonic jurisprudence.*

Masonic Jurisprudence

Why "Masonic Jurisprudence"? Why not "Masonic Law"? The latter is what is talked about most frequently. Yet, I prefer the former term. Why?

Law is more often than not set down and administered dogmatically. Too often laws are established with little study as to their affects. Once established by a group over which individuals have little or no control, they remain for years. Sometimes forever. They are administered with little regard for individual circumstances.

In a court of law, two (or more) lawyers argue before a judge what they consider the law to be. The judge determines who has the better argument, based on his experience. If the losing lawyer doesn't like the way the judge ruled, he can appeal to a higher tribunal. And he can appeal higher and higher. Law becomes what lawyers and judges say it is. Laws are contained in thousands of volumes.

Jurisprudence covers the rights of men within an organization. It becomes a study of the laws, customs, and regulations of the organization. It is designed to protect the individual.

Isn't this what "law" does? Yes and no. And there are valid arguments for both sides. We won't enter into them here. We are interested, not in civil and criminal law, but Masonic law. Or, as I prefer to call it, Masonic jurisprudence.

What is Masonic jurisprudence? It is what your Grand Lodge says it is. It's contained in one little volume—not thousands. It's something every Master Mason should study and know. And it can be learned in a short period of time. It is something that has evolved, naturally, over a period of many years. It is something that changes but little.

In the political arena, hundreds, even thousands of new laws are proposed each year. In the Grand Lodge seldom are a half-dozen proposals made to change the law. Often all of these, or most of them, are readily discarded. Unlike the political body, **every** Lodge within the jurisdictions has a voice in what is proposed. In most the proposed changes are known and studied months in advance. When the proposition comes before the delegates at the Annual Communication, they know, or should, what effect its enactment will have on the Craft.

"Masonic jurisprudence has suffered in this country for over-zealous attempts to mould our law by the analogies of the political law of the time and place." said the great Roscoe Pound over 60 years ago. He added that we should not adopt "the hasty assumption that our American legal and political institutions might be relied upon to furnish principles of law for a universal fraternity."

Fortunately, almost every Grand Lodge still bases its rules and regulations upon Anderson's Constitutions of 1723. So we have, basically, two elements of Masonic jurisprudence. The first is tradition. We still conduct Masonic affairs in the manner in which they have been handed down to us for centuries. This encompasses the experience and knowledge of countless thousands of Freemasons who have gone before us. The second composes several elements—decisions of Grand Masters, reviewed by Grand Lodges; articles on the subject, reviewed and discussed in the printed periodicals; discussions by Committees on Fraternal Correspondence.

There is yet another element, not utilized as well as it should be. This is the annual meetings of Grand Masters and Grand Secretaries. These were practically taboo in the days of Roscoe Pound, Mackey, Oliver, and the many others who have written on the subject of Masonic jurisprudence. We should look at the reasoning behind this boycott, briefly.

For two centuries there has been a great fear of the formation of a General Grand Lodge. It began in 1779 when American Union Lodge first proposed George Washington for General Grand Master. At that time there was only one independent Grand Lodge in the country. Every attempt since that time has been strongly resisted. Even when conventions for one purpose or another were called, many, if not most, Grand Lodges refused to send representatives.

With the end of World War I, a change began to take place in the thinking of many Masonic leaders. They still feared the formation of a General Grand

Lodge, but because of the efforts of a few, their fear of meeting together began to lessen. The formation of The Masonic Service Association in 1918 proved to most, but not all, that Masons could and should meet together to show their unity. This paved the way for the first Annual Conference of Grand Masters in 1925, a Conference that has continued ever since. Yet some of those attending that Conference would have nothing to do with the MSA.

Out of the Conferences of Grand Masters and Grand Secretaries, and from the MSA, have come some excellent papers on Masonic jurisprudence. Far too often these are buried. The only recipients of their worth are those in attendance. But they have had an overall effect on every Grand Lodge. Much of the thinking has found its way into decisions and recommendations of Grand Masters. This has resulted in many changes in the rules and regulations of our Grand Lodges.

Where did the laws, rules, regulations, and customs of Freemasonry come from? Mainly from Anderson's Constitutions of 1723. Surprisingly, many of these were based on **The Regis Poem** of c1390! The latter was not discovered to be a Masonic document until 1838—115 years after Anderson wrote his Constitutions. This is proof enough (for me) that Anderson didn't "manufacture" what he had "reduc'd. . . .to the ancient Records and immemorial Usages of the Fratrnity."

The Fifteen Articles and the Fifteen Points of the **Regis Poem,** plus the Charges and General Regulations, all abbreviated, will be found in **Key to Freemasonry's Growth.** These are the basis of all Masonic Jurisprudence to this day.

What follows was the keynote address for the Queen's District Leadership Seminar in 1981. From the seminar it was sent to The Masonic Service Association where it was published in The Hat and Gavel. *It was especially adapted for* The Indiana Freemason. *It's this version that appears here.*

The Ideal Lodge

The *master* Master Mason Dwight L. Smith, Past Grand Master of Masons in Indiana, provoked a discussion among several members of The Philalethes Society. That's an international Masonic research society over which Dwight was then presiding. The discussion concerned Lodges and what can make them ideal.

An ideal Lodge. That's an intriguing thought. What is it? What can it do that other Lodge's don't?

First, an ideal Lodge isn't interested in bigness. The largest Temple in the state is cold and useless if there isn't the warmth of Brotherhood in it. A numerically large membership is worthless if the members don't attend and don't participate in Masonic fellowship. A sizable bank account usually suggests the Lodge is more interested in saving for the next depression than it is in Brotherhood.

Because it's not interested in numbers only, the ideal Lodge will see that no man receives the degrees until he knows what Freemasonry is and is not. An Indoctrination Team will visit every petitioner. It will meet with him and his family. It will tell them what's expected of the man if he's accepted into the Lodge. It will answer their questions truthfully and fully. This means the fellows on this Team must be top-notch Freemasons. They must know what Freemasonry is all about. It also means some petitioners will learn this Order is not for them. It does mean that those who believe it's what they want can become the life-long-active Master Masons we should be seeking.

A word of explanation about the preference for Teams instead of Committees. There is a description of committees which is all too true: "*A committee is a group of men who, individually, can do nothing, but who can, collectively, decide that nothing can be done.*" Committees have chairmen. Usually everything is left for him to do. If he does nothing, that's what the committee does. Teams, if properly manned, work as a group. A good group can accomplish much, much more than any individual. I've proven this in many seminars.

The ideal Lodge is interested in Fellowship. So, it will have feasts and fun. Have you ever thought about why those first four Lodges in England came together? It was for a feast. For fellowship. For Brotherhood. It's only incidental that from that meeting the first Grand Lodge of speculative Masons was formed. There wasn't any mention of ritual in the early days. Members looked forward to those Masonic feasts. They wouldn't miss the opportunity of meeting with their Brothers on common ground. It was an adventure.

After the "do-gooders" turned our Masonic Lodges and Grand Lodges in this country into Puritanical gardens in the 1850's, the feasts and fun disappeared from Freemasonry in the United States. This is not so in foreign climes. In Canada and Scotland fellowship still takes first place. A Scottish Masonic leader told me when I was visiting Scotland: "The shorter the degree, the longer the harmony." Harmony is what the after Lodge get together is called. And it is fun—not Tomfoolery.

Members care for each other in the ideal Lodge. Everyone knows of the needs of everyone else. If a member is too ill to work, his fellow members will mow his lawn, do his grocery shopping, take care of the home work, and sit by his side if necessary. Whatever is needed his Brothers will provide. It will be done cheerfully. They believe in Freemasonry's First Tenet— Brotherly Love. They find nothing effeminate in one man loving another.

Let me tell you a long story briefly. Before the days of the War Between the States, Ann noted some unusual activity by her husband. He left the house at odd hours; he often took little items from their home with him, not telling her why. One night he asked her for a shawl she no longer wore. She was puzzled, but like a dutiful wife she gave it to him. The next day while she was in the village shopping, she saw a beautiful young lady wearing that shawl. Angrily she followed the girl. Into a shack walked the young lady. Not far behind went Ann, bursting through the door. She found the young lady bending over an obviously sick woman lying on a crude bed.

The woman greeted Ann with a smile. They talked. Ann learned the woman and girl had almost frozen and starved to death. Then, mysteriously, the young lady found food, coal, wood, and clothing outside the door one morning. Almost every morning since then she found the same thing. Both were regaining their health. And through some avenue just as mysterious, the young lady had been given a well-paying job.

When they had settled down after supper to their usual tasks, Ann looked at her husband and smiled. "Today," she said, "I learned the great secret of Masonry. It's to do good and not tell about it."

This is exactly what those members who belong to ideal Lodges have been doing for centuries. They have been helping others and not bragging about their good works. This is what members of ideal Lodges will continue to do for centuries to come.

The appendant bodies have been condemned and praised throughout the land. I'm not going to takes sides in this controversy. Although I belong to many Masonically related bodies, I am first, last and always a Master Mason. Nothing can take the place of Ancient Craft Masonry. If we had enough ideal Lodges we wouldn't need appendant bodies. Our members could find what they are seeking in our Lodges. They wouldn't have to look elsewhere. There was a time when this was true. When it stopped, Masons brought into existence organizations to provide what the Lodges wouldn't.

All of us are individuals. This is recognized in the ideal Lodge. Some of us want to sing. Others like drama. There are some who ride motorcycles and want to do this with a group of like-minded men. Or it might be horses. Different activities appeal to different men. We all know this. So why not encourage them to do their own thing?

Wouldn't it be fun to have a quartet in your Lodge? How about a string band? Couldn't a dramatic group provide excellent programs for your Lodge? Not to mention the District and the Jurisdiction? Wouldn't it be excellent public and internal relations for these groups to appear throughout the community? Especially if they were sponsored and supported by the ideal Lodge? What about the dozens of other activities various men are interested in? Shouldn't it be easy for a Lodge to find enough interesting things for its members to do to keep them active in the Lodge?

In widely scattered cases some of these things are now being done. But the scale is too small. Even so, where there is activity there is more than casual interest in the Lodge. Why not give it a try? Of course, there's work involved, but not too much. Especially if the leadership will delegate responsibility and authority. There's no need for the Master to lead a quartet, a dramatic group, an orchestra, or anything else. This should be delegated to the best man for the job. Then it will get done as it should. No one man can do everything. No one man knows all the answers. (This you will learn as you study more about leadership. What you learn will amaze you.)

Once you've decided you want your Lodge to be ideal, how are you going to let your members know their Lodge is once again worth attending? By telling them about it. The usual post card won't do. Neither will the "bulletin" that contains little but the names of the officers, members and committees. You're going to have to get out a newsletter. More work? Not really. Every Lodge has at least one member who knows how to write news stories. He may have been overlooked because he's not a Past Master, or even an officer. Many Masonic gems are being cast aside for this reason.

Delegate! Find the member who will write your newsletter. Tell him your goals and plans. Then let him tell the membership what those goals and plans are. The response just may surprise you. But don't expect miracles. If your Lodge has been practically dormant for years, you're not going to arouse much interest in a month. Keep the good programs rolling. Keep your members informed about what's happening, going to happen, and has happened. More and more will start attending Lodge, even if it's out of curiosity. Once you have them there, inform and entertain them—*Masonically.* Keep the civic programs out of your Lodge. Give them what they can find nowhere else—Freemasonry. If you do, your members will keep coming back.

Freemasons are hungry for Masonic information. You'll find this is true wherever you travel. It is difficult to believe that many Masons have no idea where they can find good Masonic books and material. Only a small fraction of our members know there's a Masonic Service Association ready, willing, and anxious to serve them. Most members have serious questions they want to ask, but have no way of knowing where to find the answers.

The ideal Lodge will hold periodic Study Classes. Here well-informed Brothers will impart the Masonic information the members are seeking. Here they will find the questions the ritual raises answered. Here they will be given an opportunity to give and take in the discussions. They will be asked to search in depth for some of the puzzling aspects of Freemasonry. They will be given the chance to pass along their new-found knowledge to their Brethren.

We all know ritual is important to Freemasonry. It's the first thing we encounter in our journey into Masonry. Too often it's the only thing stressed in our Lodges and Grand Lodges. It's too important to take lightly. The ideal Lodge realizes this. So, it forms ritual classes to help the ritualists to achieve perfection. It is during the conferring of the degrees the new member forms an opinion of the Craft. They are entitled to nothing but the best for the money they've paid to receive the degrees. Classes are where budding ritualists should be allowed to confer the degrees.

After our man has been raised to the Sublime Degree of Master Mason, what are we going to do with him? Are we going to let him leave without words of encouragement? Are we going to let him leave empty handed? Not if he has become a member of the ideal Lodge.

The Indoctrination Team has learned all about his likes and dislikes. It has learned what type of work he does; what his hobbies are; what special activities he enjoys. These have been cataloged and his file will be on record in the Lodge. The Master will have this file and will know exactly what to ask the new Master Mason to do. If he sings, he can become a part of this group. If he plays an instrument, the band may be where he wants to make his contribution. If he likes to cook, the stewards' Team will have a valuable addition. The important thing is to put him to work doing what he wants to do.

In the ideal Lodge the new member's endorsers will see that he attends his Lodge regularly. They will take him to other Lodges and other Masonic functions. They will see that he finds all the things Ancient Craft Masonry has to offer.

The Lodge Educational Officer, Historian, or someone designated by the Master will see that the new member has Masonic literature to read and study. He will be given a good Masonic publication before he leaves the Lodge on the night he's raised. He will be told where and how he can obtain more Masonic books and literature. In an ideal Lodge this will be no problem. It will have an excellent Masonic library.

There is plenty of work to be done in the ideal Lodge. There is no reason for any member not to have a job he will enjoy doing. Most active men aren't interested in being just a body on the sidelines. They want to participate in some way. This is one big reason so many Lodges have small attendance. Too many members don't feel they are important. The ideal Lodge will see this doesn't happen.

There's no limit to the heights the ideal Lodge can reach. There's no limit to the activities the ideal Lodge can have. All it takes is ideal Leadership to set the course.

Remember, Leadership is all-important. Study it in depth. If you will, both you and your Lodge will be the beneficiaries. So will your Grand Lodge and all Freemasonry.

This was the final presentation made at the Midwest Conference on Masonic Education held in St. Louis, Missouri, in May 1986. I was told to "don't pull any punches." I tried not to.

Innovate/Create—Or Stagnate

It Is Way Past Time For The Craft To Become Operative, Rather Than Speculative, Freemasons

"It can't be done!" is a cry we hear far too often throughout the leadership of Freemasonry. The leadership is correct. Once it has said, "It can't be done," you can bet your wife's best bonnet that it can't be done.

But—"it" can be done! Whatever "it" is or means, it can be done. Over the years a few people—innovators and creators—have proven it can be done. They were inspired by enthusiastic, motivated educators and philosophers in the dark ages, such as Aristotle, Plato, and Pythagoras. These men, and their counterparts, had ideas, shared them and the world around them improved.

Ideas

Ideas! This is the beginning of innovating and creating. Ideas. But only if they are shared. We all have them, but too often we keep them locked in our minds, and there they stay until they go off into outer space. Ideas not shared are useless. If we would only learn that each of us has only a small fraction of the knowledge available we would go a long way toward improving our lives, our country, our world, our fraternity.

When we think of ideas one man in particular comes to mind, mainly because he was honest. Thomas Edison said that he had been credited with several inventions, but only one was his alone. That was the phonograph. "I'm an awfully good sponge," he said. "I absorb ideas from every source that I can find and put them to practical use. Then I improve them until they become of some value. The ideas which I use are mostly the ideas of other people who don't develop them themselves."

107

There's a formula there that we can put to use:

- Listen for ideas
- Make notes-don't let them slip away
- Think about them
- Discuss them with others
- Develop a working model
- Improve the model
- Put them to work

What does that formula tell us? That we've got to stop shuddering and start innovating and creating.

Wallops Island, Virginia, is the site of a NASA installation that sends rockets into space. When a missile was launched into space in the early days it was likely to blow up. The cameras being used couldn't track the missiles fast enough for the pictures to determine exactly what was going wrong. A nation-wide search was made for faster cameras. None were found.

A fellow you have probably never heard of, Charles Hulcher, no novice with the space agency, had an idea one night. He thought he had found a way to move big film through a camera fast enough to do the job. He made several sketches and discussed his proposal with his boss. The boss was impressed and wanted him to go ahead with his plans. An engineer with all types of degrees said it wouldn't work. So, Hulcher's plans were dropped.

Time went by and the problems got worse. In desperation the director told Hulcher to make his camera. He did. The resulting enlarged pictures visually found the problems and brought about needed corrections.

"It can't be done," said the well-schooled, five-degree engineer. The man with no college sheepskin, but who had a practical education, dedication, and motivation, did it!

A friend of mine, who is as concerned about the decline of Freemasonry as I am, claims there is no such thing as "Masonic leadership." That our leadership is concerned only with the *status quo*. Titles, pomp and ceremony are what we seek. We're content with going through the motions and not "rocking the boat." And I'm inclined to agree with him.

The Body

It has been my observation over the past 38 years that our leadership is overly obsessed with ritual. Ritual is important. There would be no Freemasonry without it. But it is certainly not the alpha and omega of the Craft. If our leadership will understand this, many of our woes will be ended.

As I see it, the "Body of Freemasonry" consists of six parts. I depicted this in a drawing that appeared in the first edition of the late *The Altar Light* in June 1977. The parts:

- Ritual = skeleton (or framework)
- Bloodstream = philosophy

- Muscles = jurisprudence
- Flesh = history (or binder)
- Soul = benevolence
- Brain and heart = symbolism

Which of these parts is the most important? Each of them. Which can we live without? The answer, of course, is none of them. Yet, we have been feeding the demigod called "Ritual" abundantly while keeping the other vital parts of the body alive by what doctors call "heroic means." A few, darn few, Freemasons are providing nourishment for the rest of the body.

And we wonder why we are stagnating!

Throughout Freemasonry, with rare exceptions, where is most of the money collected from the membership spent? First, for another of our demigods called "Annual Communications"; Second, for our chief demigod, "Ritual." To keep our ritual pure and unadulterated it costs us a goodly percentage of our budget. The ritualists dine on steak; the rest, on grape jelly sandwiches.

Can there be dedication without education? I don't think so. Yet we expect men to be dedicated to the principles of Freemasonry without knowing anything about the fraternity except the ritual.

The ritual our Operative Brethren practiced, if we can believe the exposés and Old Gothic Constitutions, was indeed small. They were more interested in education, learning what the tools of their trade were and how to use them, thereby enabling them to improve themselves in masonry. For the past two centuries we Speculative Masons haven't cared what the tools were. So we haven't learned how to use them.

Today we appoint men to committees and give them no direction. We appoint men as educators who know little or nothing about the Craft, except how to dot the "i's" and cross the "t's" in the demigod we call ritual. These men are told to go forth and Masonically educate the masses. The masses are crying for knowledge, but they obviously can't obtain it from men who probably know less than they do.

Re-Inventing The Wheel

We can take several lessons from the Israel Air Force. It accepts only the best of the best. It spends the money and the time necessary to teach and train its men. Only one out of ten make the grade. But those who don't are not discarded. They become members of the "second team." A country as small as Israel can't afford to discard anyone with motivation and capability. Freemasonry can't afford to throw them away, either.

This air force buys the best equipment and makes it better. It purchases American manufactured planes and adds innovative accessories to those planes to make them better than they were. They don't re-invent the wheel; they improve on what they get.

If we would stop burying our heads in the sands of oblivion we would do the same thing. Educational conferences have been held throughout the country for decades, among the best and the oldest is this Midwest Conference. Year after year good proposals are suggested, along with plans to implement them. Many of these same proposals are made year after year, not only here but in other conferences. We continue to invent the wheel. We waste time and money. We discourage those who, like Edison, take ideas, develop them, present them, only to have them thrown away through ignorance.

Educational Conferences

But let's take a hard look at conferences such as the Midwest and Northeast Conferences. Have they done the job they were expected to do? You be the judge. The hard-hitting, searching questions I'll leave for you to ask and answer.

Recently I was given two hours by a Grand Lodge to discuss leadership with the Masters and Wardens of its jurisdiction. At the outset I made it clear that we could barely touch on the subject, and the only way we would accomplish anything was with participation. If they asked questions and shared their knowledge, we would accomplish something. That's rather difficult when there are 450 present, but they did.

It wasn't at all surprising to me to find that many of these fellows were hungry for knowledge. The one thing that kept cropping up was why didn't the Grand Lodge hold such workshops often. Each time this was mentioned there was applause. But it also wasn't surprising to me to find that the Grand Lodge leadership ignored these pleas. Why?

Because it takes time and money to do a job the way it's supposed to be done. It also takes knowledgeable Masons to handle questions from the floor. It's much easier to make a speech of sorts, bow to the applause and sit down. But how many will remember ten words the speaker spoke? How many of you will remember anything I've said or will say?—Unless it's something that rubs a sore spot.

Something For Nothing

This brings us to another demigod in our fraternity that has helped us stagnate. Its called "demanding something for nothing." We're not about to spend one cent more than we have to for anything except the over-blown annual communications of our Grand Bodies.

That is, we're not about to pay a Freemason for anything he does for the fraternity. He's expected to give of us time, talent and money because of his love for the Craft. And we wonder why we don't have more outstanding speakers, writers, dramatists, educators, and others with talent working with and for us. Have you ever thought about why the ritual is a demigod? It's because that's where the money is being spent.

For years I've been suggesting, sometimes rather strongly, that we must have full time Masonic educators. To have them we must be prepared to pay them a living wage—not Masters' wages. Today there is only one such person in all Freemasonry in the United States. Has he been successful? Again you be the judge. His jurisdiction rarely, if ever, has a loss in membership.

The late Harold V.B. Voorhis, who spent almost seven decades working for Freemasonry in all in branches, in his *Facts For Freemasons,* claimed that I am the foremost Masonic educator in the country. If this is so, we are in sad shape indeed.

Suggestions

I'd like to say I have the solution to our woes, but I've always tried to be honest, so I can't make that claim. I can, however, offer some suggestions that just might lead us toward the solution. Here they are:
- Let's take the ritual off its pedestal and arm it with the implements of progress. These include all the elements of good management, which we can call Constructive Leadership. Here are those elements:
- Define the PURPOSE
- Set GOALS to achieve the purpose
- Establish PLANS to reach the goals
- Continually COMMUNICATE with all concerned
- STAFF the Teams of workers properly
- ORGANIZE the staff to achieve results
- CONTROL the action

Each of these points is crucial to successfully accomplishing anything. Each should be studied and discussed at length. It can't be done in the short space alloted here. Nor is it possible to teach anyone the fundamentals of leadership in an hour or two. I've written books and hundreds of articles on this subject. It took more than an hour or two to do that.

Which brings me to a point I've mentioned and will now emphasize. The type of educational conferences, workshops, and seminars we have been conducting are a waste of time and money. You cannot develop teachers, or leaders, in an hour or two. You cannot do it the way we've been trying to do it for decades.

Too many of us are in love with the sound of our own voices. Too many of us believe we know all the answers to everything. That's because too many of us are egotists! If that adds sandpaper instead of salve to earlier wounds— good. It just may make us think.

YOUR goal may mean nothing to me, or anyone else. If you let me, or those who will be involved, help you set your goal, we will then be committed to helping you achieve it.

YOUR plans may be the best possible, but if those who will be involved in carrying them out are ignored, your plans will be shunned, also. The same holds true for everything YOU consider alone.

What am I stressing? That there must be PARTICIPATION. With participation you can accomplish much; without it, little.

Let me stress a point that goes along with participation. Take the time and the money to teach teachers to teach those willing to learn. To do it you and they will need

- The proper tools;
- The materials necessary;
- Time.

The tools will include audio-visual aids, something Freemasonry is ignoring. The materials will include books, articles, handouts and other information. To cover a minimum of instruction will take at least a couple of weekends. Anything less is time wasted.

Frankly, I believe that most of you know what should be done, but too many of us have said nothing. We

- Are afraid to "rock the boat."
- Won't ask for the money necessary.

We're afraid we might make the "bosses" angry and destroy our chances for a promotion. We don't want to appear to be aggressive and ask for money because this might anger the "bosses." In short, fear is the culprit that has been helping Freemasonry to stagnate, that keeps us from innovating and creating.

Where's the money to come from, you might ask? From one of the demigods of Freemasonry—the annual communication. Most of you have attended more Grand annual meetings than I have. But few of you have read more annual *Proceedings* than I have. I have yet to find an annual meeting that could not have been conducted in less than one-half the time scheduled. That would make them far less boring.

Then, too, if we provide significant seminars the participants won't mind paying for them. Those of you, like me, who receive dozens of "invitations" to attend seminars know these cost anywhere from $300 per person a half-day up into the thousands.

We can, if we will, provide excellent workshops and seminars for a fraction of that cost.

Conclusion

I'm not one who goes in for poetry for a serious address. But I want to conclude as I began, and no one has said it better than Brother Edgar A. Guest, an early Fellow of The Philalethes Society.

Somebody said that it couldn't be done,
  But he with a chuckle replied
That "maybe it couldn't," but he would be one
  Who wouldn't say so till he'd tried.
So he buckled right in with the trace of a grin
  On his face. If he worried he hid it.
He started to sing as he tacked the thing
  That couldn't be done, and he did it.

Let me suggest, "just buckle in with a bit of a grin, Just take off your coat and go to it; Just start to sing as you tackle the thing That 'cannot be done,' and you'll do it."

Good luck. And may God go with you.

Several questions followed. Here are some of them.

Q. What is the best method of desseminating information for Lodge education?

A. Workshops and seminars over a weekend or longer.

Q. Yet you say, with that method, within ten minutes after they have had this instruction they forget it.

A. No, not instruction—speeches. Speeches are the downfall of our Masonic education. Participation, not speeches, will accomplish what we're seeking. It takes more than an hour or two if there is to be meaningful participation. It will take time and money. This is what we won't spend—time and money.

Q. Do you have handouts to go along with these workshops? Audio-visual is only 50% of your instruction because you don't retain it. I feel you must have published material along with it.

A. Sure you do. You must have handouts; you must have the whole nine yards. But don't discount audio-visual teaching. People retain about 80% of what they see and hear; only 10%, if that much, of what they hear alone.

Q. Why isn't this room full? Why is it that men will take the time to learn the ritual and yet they will not take the time to learn about Masonry?

A. Because the ritual is required, knowing something about Freemasonry isn't. This is the case in Virginia and I assume almost everywhere else.

Q. (Rather, statement.) When the Worthy Grand Matron went to Illinois on two occasions the armory was rented. There were 250 to 300 people there to listen to this gracious lady speak for forty minutes and say nothing. At a lodge meeting last night there were 35. And look at the attendance here. Is it because we aren't paying enough, we aren't rewarding enough, we aren't giving enough incentives to cause people to come to something like this?

A. It could be. But you've struck a responsive chord. Many in our Masonic leadership don't believe women have any place in Freemasonry. Yet I know many men who won't go in line because their wives won't let them. I know other men who have had to drop out because their wives made them. Women do have a strong influence on what we do in Freemasonry. This could be one of the reasons the Eastern Star meetings were packed—the husbands *had to go with their wives.* I strongly believe we've let another important ingredient slip away from us. We must put *fun* back into Freemasonry.

Q. How do we go about soliciting suggestions and ideas within the framework of a very traditionally oriented organization that tends to stifle the very thing you are asking for?

A. It doesn't stifle it—unless we let it.

Q. (Statement.) But we do let it! That's the problem.

A. We address this "problem" in one of my films, *Breaking Barriers to*

Communication which features the late Conrad Hahn. In speaking of organizational realities we claim these are few, but if we don't want to do anything we use those few as a crutch to do nothing. We have a lot of crutches and it's very easy to use them.

Q. (Statement.) I agree with most of what you have said, but we are a little bit off on the ritual. I am a ritualist, a Grand Lecturer. We do emphasize the ritual, but we put emphasis on other programs. Running down the ritual is counter-productive.

A. Let me make this point clear. I do not downgrade the ritual. I happen to be a good ritualist. I have been President of a Masonic Traveling Degree Team for 24 years. I happen to know all the ritual there is in Virginia. I have conducted more Masonic funerals than any man in my lodge ever has, living or dead. From memory I have installed officers in several lodges many times. I know the ritual, but I also know that we are treating it as the beginning and end of all Freemasonry. As long as we do that, as long as we let the ritualists control Freemasonry, particularly our Grand Lodges, we are in trouble. The ritualists aren't interested in leaders who don't dot every "i" and cross every "t." This is a big mistake.

Q. I agree with you. Let's develop good programs and use the ritual to develop the rest of it.

A. Let's do that. But let's do the same for education as we do for the ritual. Let's get paid directors of Masonic education, public relations, and whatever. Let's get one man who can coordinate everything in each jurisdiction. Let's pay him a living wage so he can formulate plans and put them to work. Let's do this in every jurisdiction in the United States and you will witness Freemasonry's rebirth.

The Grand Lodge of Georgia held a leadership conference near Atlanta in August 1985. This is the paper I presented.

Developing Leadership

For the past several weeks I've been asking questions about what I should discuss with you today. The answers have been anything but enlightening. Several said I should tell you to read my book, *Key To Freemasonry's Growth,* and then sit down! Others said I should tell you to join The Philalethes Society—then quit!

These are good suggestions. *Key* tells us how to use the principles of management within Freemasonry; The Philalethes Society has the best Masonic publication available. Among other pertinent items, it continually runs articles about leadership in some form. But I'm sure those answers were meant to be facetious. Those fellows knew I had to do better than that.

In one of my training films, which many of you in Georgia have seen, I asked a question that's rarely considered: Which comes first, education or dedication?

If we were conducting a seminar, and I wish we were, you would be participating in this discussion. We'd have a large tear pad on an easel and we'd get your input. We don't have the pad, but any time you want to hoot, howl, boo, or whatever, feel free to do it. I firmly believe the only way we can learn anything is through participation.

Which does come first—education or dedication? To me it must be education. How can we expect anyone to be dedicated to something he knows nothing about? How good would a plumber be without years of apprenticeship? Would you ask a man to defend you in a court of law merely because he was a good mechanic? Would you ask a lawyer to cut a tumor out of your brain because he was a good friend of yours?

Of course you wouldn't. But every day we turn over some important aspects of Freemasonry to someone who knows absolutely nothing about the Craft. We do it to reward friendship, or a "good ole Boy." This is one of the big reasons the Fraternity has all types of problems.

115

In last week's edition of *InfoWorld* the editor lamented the lack of knowledge in the commercial world. He wanted to purchase an expensive automobile. He found a salesman who knew nothing about the car he was interested in. After an hour or so he left in disgust.

Several letters in the same magazine condemned a chain of well-known stores for having clerks who know nothing. Computer software firms came in for their share of criticism. Many are selling programs they know are loaded with faults. Amazingly, these software manufacturers are getting away with warranties that promise nothing—not even that their programs will work— and you can't get your money back if they don't!

Can we draw an analogy here with Freemasonry? Do we promise our petitioners and members anything? Are we taking them into Lodges where there is faulty work? Are we providing them with Masonic programs that are worthy of their time? When was the last time you heard of a dissatisfied Mason getting his money back?

A couple of months ago I ate in a large restaurant. When I went to pay my bill the cashier didn't know how to operate the cash register. I showed her how. Then she didn't know how to make change. I helped her. The lack of training was disgusting. How could any business put an employee to work without educating him or her?

But, don't we do this in Freemasonry continually? How many Masters do you know who have learned anything about the Craft beyond the ritual? How many know the Masonic law as it pertains to this jurisdiction? How many understand Masonic protocol? Symbolism? Benevolence? Or the history of Masonry?

Aren't we inclined to select men who are popular to start in the line in our Lodges. They don't rock the boat; they go along with the *status quo*? Isn't the same thing done in almost every Grand Lodge in the country?

Why do we do this? Because we don't realize we're jeopardizing the greatest fraternal organization the world has ever known. We don't believe that, like any business, Freemasonry can become bankrupt.

If you don't believe this you haven't been reading the *Proceedings* of Grand Lodges.

The list of our woes can go on for hours. But you know what many of them are. You don't need me to waste your time enumerating them. So, let's take a few minutes to try to determine how we can turn our problems into triumphs.

Constructive Leadership can reverse the trend toward oblivion.

It isn't too late to develop the Constructive Leadership we must have. If I thought it was I wouldn't have gotten up at four this morning to be here today. It's not too late, even though the overwhelming majority of our active Masons are well over forty. This was graphically illustrated at an assembly of York Rite Masons I addressed about a month ago. Those over sixty were asked to stand. Of the more than 200 there, three-fourths stood. Then those forty or under were asked to do the same. Two stood!

There's a tremendous lesson here. Those of us who are past our prime must move to the front in becoming Constructive Leaders. We must believe

116

the old cliché that one is never too old to learn. We must learn so we can teach.

Most of you, if not all of you, have benefited from "post-graduate study." You have participated in high priced seminars, or workshops, intended to make you more proficient in your business or profession. Some of the cost was paid by you; most of it was paid by your company. Usually this money was well-spent. You and your company reaped many benefits.

There are further lessons here for Freemasonry, lessons that we've ignored. We take good men, give them a job to do, but without the training and tools they must have. We won't spend the money necessary. We are so short-sighted we believe everything we do for Masonry should be done for free. Then we wonder why many good writers, speakers and educators who are Master Masons do nothing for the Craft.

Many times I've said THERE IS NOTHING MORE EXPENSIVE THAN IGNORANCE. I've also claimed that Freemasonry has the greatest leaders of industry, business, politics, trades and the professions in the world. Most of them have ignored the Craft for varying reasons. One reason is because we're penny-pinchers; another is because of the mediocre leadership we find too often.

We can reverse this trend by using the principles of good management.

It would take hours, if not days, to cover these principles and how to make them work. All we can do here is touch upon them. But if a responsive cord is struck in you, there are many ways you can build on this discussion.

First we must have a mission—a purpose for the existence of the organization. We're discussing Freemasonry, so this is what we'll concentrate on. If I asked you to share your thinking on this purpose, you would have many. And rightly so. Although we claim we have but one purpose — to make good men better. There are dozens of other reasons for our existence, but this one is worthy of our consideration.

Once we've determined our PURPOSE—our mission—we must have GOALS to carry out this mission. To reach these goals we must make PLANS. For plans to be successful there must be meaningful COMMUNI-CATION. We must know something about ORGANIZING—or Staffing. We must learn how to CONTROL everything every step along the way toward reaching our goals to achieve our purpose.

This isn't easy. But, as with everything worthwhile, being a leader isn't supposed to be easy.

We use these principles of management in our pursuit of a livelihood every day. Why don't we use them in Freemasonry? Because Masonry is a non-profit organization, we say, and it doesn't need the same rules of management. But, is it, or any organization, a non-profit association?

Actually, what is profit? In its simplest form it's BENEFITS DERIVED OR RECEIVED less UNWANTED CONSIDERATIONS. In the business world this would be interpreted to mean income less expenses equals net profit. In organizations such as ours, if the undesirable considerations are less than the benefits offered, we have a profit. This "profit" translates into more dedicated Master Masons and a good public and internal image.

If we want to increase our "profits" in the Craft we must start employing the principles of good management (and these are really the ingredients for Constructive Leadership). These are:

1. We must set goals.
2. We must establish plans to reach those goals.
3. We must develop meaningful communication.
4. We must learn how to organize, or staff, our Lodges and Grand Lodges (that means to select the right men for the right job).
5. We must learn how to control the plans and staff to reach the goals.

I fully realize we can, and should, spend several hours discussing each of these steps. We don't have that time, so let me hope that I've planted a seed or two and you will pursue this subject in your spare time.

But I want to leave one last, and most important, subject with you. This is leadership. Without leadership what I've been saying is doomed. So, without question, we must develop *Constructive* Leadership. You'll note, I'm emphasizing *Constructive* Leadership.

In one of my films I point out that Andy Capp, the creation of the English cartoonist, Reggie Smythe, is a leader. He knows how to get things done through other people as a good leader must. It's usually his wife. He has never worked a day in his life. He lives off the public dole, and what his wife earns. He's a leader all right, but not one I'd call Constructive.

We have many of the same type of leaders in our Lodges and Grand Lodges. When something progressive is proposed, they will stand up and support the action with pious phrases. Then they will throw so many stumbling blocks in the way the proposal is defeated. These are the men who never had an original idea of their own. They aren't about to see the ideas of others adopted or tried. These are the round pegs in the square holes. They are the men who make it difficult to keep constructive leaders. Rather than continue to fight these men, the constructive leader goes where his efforts will be appreciated.

We must develop Constructive Leaders. But where are we going to find them?

I knew of one of them in your jurisdiction over 20 years ago. Your then Grand Master shared a table with my wife and me at our Grand Master's banquet. He didn't know this man, but after I had told him of many of his attributes, your Grand Master said he'd check him out when he returned home. He did. Two weeks later he was made a member of your Historical and Education Committee. He later became Editor of your publication. He worked long and hard for Freemasonry in general. Shortly before he died he became the first to receive your highest award. He was my good friend Walter M. Callaway, Jr.

Such potential leaders are all around us. Too often, however, these are the men we've been warned against. They aren't the type of men who "go by the book." They know how to circumvent the obstructions the "book" often places on progress. They are goal-oriented rather than task- oriented. They look for constructive criticism so they can improve. They seek responsibility, the greater the better. They are creative; they'll use ideas and work to make them succeed. But if they fail they'll go on to something else.

Problems are something every leader must face. The Constructive Leader takes them in stride. He looks forward to solving them. He'll initiate action without the fear of failure. He knows you can't accomplish something if you don't try. Once he is given a job to do, he wants to be left alone to accomplish the task. He'll seek advice as every good leader will, but he'll weigh that advice before using it. He'll continually adjust to the reality of every situation. He knows nothing remains static. Adjustments are always necessary.

The Constructive Leader enjoys what he does. He'll "radiate the joy of wisdom," as Conrad Hahn once expressed it. The Constructive Leader will make us know that there's fun in being a Freemason.

We have forgotten that Speculative Freemasonry didn't come into being as a straight-laced, somber, ritualistic association. It was organized around the festive board. There was little, if any, ritual. There was Brotherhood, friendship, and fun.

We must put the "fun" back into the Fraternity. We will if we want to develop the Constructive Leadership we must have if we are to survive.

There's no limit to the heights to which this greatest fraternal organization in the world can rise if we will quickly, and honestly, attempt to develop Constructive Leadership.

Personally Speaking

The lessons taught in Freemasonry are as old as life itself. They are age-less. Yet they are as modern as the 21st century. They aren't superficial. They are deep and profound. Perhaps this is the reason so few of us ever learn them. But those who do are blessed.

The lessons aren't learned, perhaps, because too many of us are too busy earning coin of the realm. Perhaps it's because these lessons won't make our life easier to live. In fact, they just might make life tougher. They could consume time we could spend becoming wealthy or famous.

So, why would anyone want to dig into the mysteries of Freemasonry? Why should we expect any man to be so foolish? Why do a few become absorbed in the teachings and principles of the Craft while the majority don't?

I've asked myself these questions for more than thirty-five years. Others have been asking them for much longer. How can they be answered? How can we justify the hundreds of hours devoted to the Craft, often neglecting our families, our friends, our business?

Each individual will have his own answers. These will be almost as numer-ous as the individuals answering them. I'm not about to presume to respond for anyone else. Nor will I pretend I can even offer an explanation for myself.

Perhaps it's because we can find an inner-peace in the lessons we learn in our lodges. On many occasions I've gone to my lodge, or some other, feeling depressed. Things in the outer world had been disillusioning for varying reasons. It took some effort to drag myself out of the house. Once in the lodge the depression evaporated. Why?

Maybe it was because of the fellowship. More likely it was because I had entered another world; a world of centuries ago; a world which I was sharing today with Master Masons of years long gone. I was a small part of that select fraternity of men who shared a philosophy that can only be found in Freemasonry. I participated in a simple ritual that carried me back hundreds of years. A ritual great and ordinary men had shared. I was sharing my life with millions who came before me and I might leave a little something for the millions who will follow.

Every stage of my Masonic life is deeply etched in my mind. I can remember the Masons I knew in my childhood and how I wanted to be like them. I joined an organization when I was eighteen called "The Royal Arcanum" because I was told it was similar to Masonry. It was I would later find out. In this organization I became a "Regent," that's similar to a Worshipful Master. Then the big war came along and I enlisted in the Navy. When that was over I made my home in Virginia. I asked my wife's boss, a 32nd degree Scottish Rite Mason, how I could become a Mason. Six months later I asked him again. He finally admitted he didn't know. Then we moved to Highland Springs.

At church one day I told a fellow I knew to be a member: "I've always wanted to be a Mason, but I guess you Masons don't like me." He looked peculiar and asked: "Why do you say that?"

"Because none of you have ever asked me to be one," I told him. He laughed: "No one ever will, but now that you've asked I'll see what I can do." That afternoon I had a petition!

The lodge elected me to receive the First Degree, then personal problems developed. I had opened a small bakery using all but one War Bond to finance it. That one bond had been saved to pay my fees. My wife, Dottie, fell on some ice causing her to lose our baby. We had no hospitalization insurance. But she wouldn't let me use that one bond. "You've been saving that so you could become a Mason," she said. The fellows in the lodge offered to postpone my initiation, but Dottie wouldn't let them.

The night of my Initiation I was a nervous wreck! No one tried to calm my fears about what was going to happen. That's something that should always be done. My first moments in the lodge didn't help any. But this soon changed. Someone prayed. Then the Master assured me I had nothing to fear. From that moment to this I found something I had been seeking—an inner-peace that money can't buy.

As I listened to the men, some with familiar voices, recite the ritual I became more and more impressed. When I started to learn the catechism I was overwhelmed. I asked questions about what certain words and phrases meant. My coach didn't know the answers. This was disturbing. He wasn't alone. I couldn't find anyone in my lodge who could answer the questions. Oh, they knew the ritual letter-perfect, but what the ritual meant was a mystery to them.

As I progressed through the three degrees I became deeply engrossed in what I was hearing. My questions continued and I became more and more frustrated. The ritualistic renditions were perfect. The ritualists were impressive. The words were beautiful. Many I could readily understand, but I couldn't find the answers to those with which I wasn't familiar.

Even so, the ritual was so intriguing I learned all the lectures given by the Master during my first year. This appeared to disturb some "old-timers." They claimed I was too ambitious and they would make certain I was never elected to the line! I wasn't. For nine years I was nominated for Junior Deacon and was defeated. But in my tenth year I was elected Senior Deacon!

During those ten years I taught many candidates the necessary catechisms. But, during those first years, like those who had taught me, I couldn't give them any explanation for the words they had to learn.

During this period I learned about The Masonic Service Association. A letter to Carl H. Claudy, the Executive Secretary, brought me a wealth of information about the meaning within the ritual of Freemasonry. I also learned there were several good Masonic libraries from which I could borrow books. My favorite quickly became the library of the Grand Lodge of Iowa.

Since then I've tried to devote as much time as possible to letting the Masonic world know there is literature available. In doing this I've provided some of this literature.

Perhaps I shouldn't be surprised, but I am. It's disturbing to know as many today don't know where to find good Masonic books, pamphlets, booklets, and so on, as there were when I started looking. I find few lodges with libraries. There are few Freemasons who read Masonic books. It is claimed a Masonic book becomes a Masonic best seller if 5,000 copies are sold. And there are over six million Masons in the world!

After I discovered the world of Masonic literature a whole new universe opened for me. As I learned more and more about the Craft, the more I wanted to learn. Long ago I found the best way to learn was to share your knowledge and ideas with others. So I accepted speaking engagements. Then I began writing for Masonic periodicals.

Joining Virginia Research Lodge was one of the many joys I've found in membership in the Craft. Masonic papers were always needed and welcomed. This turned me into something of a researcher.

My first book was the result of a paper I started to prepare for Research Lodge. The story of Freemasonry and the Civil War had never been covered. Because of a story told by a minister during a Masonic church service I believed a beautiful account could be found. The paper I started turned into *House Undivided*. With the publication of this book my life was changed.

Would I give up my membership in Freemasonry? Absolutely not! Oh, there have been times, many of them, when I've thrown up my hands and said I'm quitting. Then I remembered the system and its perfection. It's far superior to any individual. Individuals come and go, are good and weak, nasty and loving. This system called "Freemasonry" rises above us all.

The York Rite Bodies meet in a central location in Maryland for what they call the "August Scene." The Masonic leadership of the state and surrounding area is urged to attend. In 1986 I was invited to be one of the guest speakers. What I said was published in The Royal Arch Mason *Autumn, 1987. This is an abbreviated version, some of what I said then is found in other chapters in this book. It might be well to mention here that often the leadership of these conferences requests me to emphasize points I've covered in other arenas. The repetition becomes mandatory.*

LET THERE BE LIGHT
In the beginning God created the Heavens and the Earth, and the Earth was without form and void, and darkness rested upon the face of the deep, and God said: "Let there be light!" And there was light.

Every Freemason is familiar with this phrase. Every Freemason has heard it while on his knees before a sacred altar. Every Freemason has been brought to light, abruptly, as the blindfold is whipped from his eyes.

At this point I can sit down if all of you are among the five percent of our members who love the ritual, particularly if you are among those who believe there is nothing in Freemasonry beyond the ritual. But, I've been assured you are among the 95% of us who believe we must be masonically educated. I've been assured you are in the group that's seeking more light. I've also been assured you are among the leaders of Freemasonry in Maryland. So, let me continue.

On being brought to light, what does our candidate behold? First the Holy Bible, or another sacred Book if he is of a religion other than Christianity. He next sees the Square and Compasses with the aid of three lighted tapers, and these are explained to him. As he looks up he sees the Master walking toward him, through a wall of men that looks like a tunnel. Then he has more ritual recited to him.

Our new Freemason has been brought to light—or has he? Does he ever get away from the "tunnel" he saw when he looked toward the East? Or will he, along with most of those who attend our lodges continue to have "tunnel vision?"

125

There are many definitions for "tunnel vision"—narrow-minds, seeing only what we want to see, looking at a field in a wide world, never being able to see the whole picture because our vision is focused on one small segment.

All of us look at life through restricted windows. Our view is restricted because of what we learned in our childhood from our parents, the schools we attended, the places we worshipped, our friends, our neighbors and neighborhood, our places of employment, the associations to which we belong, or don't belong. And the list can go on and on.

The one place that should defeat the curse of tunnel vision and broaden the outlook, by taking away the restrictions from our windows, is Freemasonry. Does it do the job it's supposed to?

Freemasonry does, but we, the individuals who are responsible for seeing that it does, don't. We have gotten away, far away, from the teachings of our founding fathers. We have taken the word "speculative" and added it to our vocabulary when we should have left in the word "operative."

Why have we done it? Because we have turned to new gods whom we call "ritualists." Don't get me wrong. I'll never belittle the need for good ritualists, because without them we could have no system called "Freemasonry." They are an essential part of the system, and I happen to be a darned good ritualist. But our tunnel vision far too often causes us to look no further than the ritual.

[At this point I mentioned some of my early frustration in an attempt to learn more about the Craft.]

In an interview in 1962, Henry Wilson Coil was asked what he was going to write about next concerning Freemasonry. He said: "There is nothing left. Now that Allen Roberts has written about Masonry during the Civil War, nothing is left to write about!"

Not too strangely, Coil wrote several books after that—and I wrote 17 more books and a countless number of articles. He learned the things to be told about Freemasonry will never end. As we gain more light in Masonry we'll add to the knowledge we now have. Perhaps most important, future writers and historians will vastly improve on what we have done.

But where are the future writers and historians to come from?

This was a concern of Raymond Rideout, Grand Master of Masons in Maine, in 1961. He asked me to address the subject at the Northeast Conference on Masonic Education when it was held in Maine in 1962. I claimed then that in Freemasonry we had few real editors, although we did have many dedicated Freemasons attempting to be editors. We had even fewer authors; we had only a handful of Masons writing articles.

I asked why? Why do we have few professional editors, writers and authors? The answer was simple: Freemasonry offers its dedicated workers little or no "coin of the realm." All who work for the Craft are expected to do it because of love. Unfortunately, a man raising a family and building a home, cannot feed the family or pay for the home with his love for Freemasonry. So, if he's a professional writer, the kind we must have, he's going to use his time profitably.

Naturally, there are exceptions here, as there are in every case. But there aren't enough exceptions to do the job that needs to be done if Freemasonry is to prosper. I noted then that Masonic editors are the most poorly paid writers in the world. Twenty-four years later, they still are. Consequently, today we have even fewer Masonic editors than we had in 1962. As for writers, they never have been paid anything. This holds true today. We have fewer writers now than we had in 1962.

Yesterday I learned that a non-Mason has been hired by a large Grand Lodge on a full time basis to write its history. Why wasn't a Freemason hired to do the job? I can't answer that, but the Grand Lodge says its because the man, not being a Mason is expected to add "objectivity" to its story. Another Grand Lodge has hired two professors who aren't Freemasons to write its history.

If we are to spread the light of Freemasonry, which is even more important today than it was a quarter century ago, we must have excellent Masonic writers.

If there is to be more light in Freemasonry we must have more and better Masonic speakers. The civic clubs, the colleges, the entertainment arena wouldn't consider inviting a good speaker to address their group for free. If you don't believe this, you can easily check it out. What do we offer our Masonic speakers? Almost always—nothing. You can easily check this out, also.

Gas guzzling vehicles cost just as much to run for Masonic speakers as they do for others. Masonic speakers aren't allowed to travel by air gratis. They pay just as much as others. Hotels don't give Masons a discount. It costs them just as much for food as it does for others. It takes as much time, if not more, for Masonic speakers to prepare an address. Yet, rarely does a Masonic speaker receive a reimbursement for even his out-of-pocket expenses.

Isn't it strange? We claim we are seeking more and more light in Masonry, yet we quibble about pennies. Isn't it strange? We have the greatest leaders of industry, professions, trades, governments, and everything else within our ranks throughout the country, and even the free world. We have leaders who never hesitate to spend the money necessary to educate those whom they lead in the secular world. Yet, make them Masonic leaders and the purse strings are knotted tightly. That is, unless non- Masons are hired to do what Freemasons have to do for free.

These same leaders spend millions of dollars every year educating their workers. They don't hesitate to provide or send their managers and workers to seminars costing hundreds of dollars per person. Yet, they won't spend a dime to provide the needed education for members of the Craft. If you don't believe me, you can easily check this out also. Search the *Proceedings* of any Masonic body for the amount of money spent on Masonic education. You'll be shocked.

"Let there be light!" we proclaim. Yet we have done little or nothing to bring the light of Freemasonry blazing forth. We elect and appoint men to positions they know little or nothing about. Most of these men want to do a job, but we don't help them. We don't provide them with the tools, the money, or the knowledge they must have to do the job they are appointed to. How can there be light?

It's not too late to start winning the battle, but time is running out. You don't have to check this out. All you have to do is consider the attacks on Freemasonry running rampant today. Many of you watched, as I did, one of your own turncoats give a graphic illustration of the degrees of Freemasonry on national television. You listened to him denounce the Craft as "unChristian." You heard his weak argument inviting Master Masons to renounce their Masonry and warn the uninitiated to stay out. Don't think for a moment this, and the hundreds of other attacks, aren't hurting us.

Recently our Philalethes Chapter invited a Mason-hating preacher to address our group to tell us why we shouldn't be Freemasons. He preached the same old bunk we've heard over and over again. During the question and answer period we had him tied in knots. But, unfortunately, the average Mason wasn't there, and no un-initiated will ever learn how vulnerable these Mason-haters are.

Let me assure you of one thing: You can't whip these fellows on their own turf. Should any of us appear on a television program with them, the positive reaction to Freemasonry will be edited out. But you can be certain the fluffs will be emphasized.

Isn't it time for some Grand Lodge or other Grand body to sue one or more of these bigots for slander, defamation, or libel? When they call us disciples of Satan, practitioners of Satanism, unChristian, unreligious, and make dozens of other foul and false claims, we have a multi-million dollar law suit. We have some of the most brilliant attorneys within our Craft, lawyers who could easily prove the falsity of these liars in a court of law. Why don't we sue? Quite frankly, I firmly believe it will take only one suit to put a stop to the anti-Masonic diatribe. Is there a better method of stopping these liars from dimming the light of Freemasonry? Is there a better way to keep the light of Freemasonry burning brightly?

Since the beginning of time there has been a war raging. Battle after battle has been fought for the minds of men. With the latest in electronic equipment, the battles have increased. Our enemies have used this modern equipment to fight these battles. Freemasonry has ignored this equipment. Why?

Because it costs money! We aren't about to spend a penny more than we have to, except to keep our ritual "pure." We are ignoring the fact that ignorance is not bliss, it's expensive, so expensive it will lose us the battle for our existence before many more decades have become history.

What can we do to save this only fraternal organization that truly believes in the Brotherhood of Man under the Fatherhood of God?

Remove the shackles and blinders. Loosen our purse strings. Give the 95% of our members what they are seeking—Freemasonry along with the ritual.

Over and over again I've heard the claim: "We don't have the money!" Hogwash! Give the 95% of our members something other than the ritual and worrying about money will be a thing of the past. Even so, there's a ready supply of funds available now. We merely have to cut the boring, and non-productive, annual meetings in half. If we do millions of dollars throughout Freemasonry can be put to constructive use.

Let us stop appointing men to do jobs they don't know how to do. Let us teach the teachers how to teach the masses. Then give the teachers the tools and funds they must have to do the job we expect them to do.

Give the newly Raised Mason something to take home other than a Holy Bible. He undoubtedly has more than one copy of this or he wouldn't have become a Freemason. When he leaves his Lodge on the night he has become a member of the Craft, he's bewildered by what he has heard and seen. If he's the type of man we're seeking, he wants to learn more about this organization of which he's now a member. Start him on this road to knowledge by giving him at least one good Masonic book. He'll take it from there.

Form study groups. Let the new member and the older ones meet in an informal atmosphere to discuss Freemasonry, openly and freely. Use good Masonic books as the vocal point. Discuss their contents. Expand on what they say. Find good leaders to conduct leadership seminars and workshops. Use audio/visual aids for illustrating points. Then watch the leadership improve.

Will this work? You can safely bet your next week's allowance that it will. It has been proven over and over again. But it takes time. You cannot hold a two hour conference of speakers once a year and expect results. All you do with this is whet the appetites of those who want more. But you must have something other than speeches that are as dry as last winter's leaves. You must have participation.

In 1976 we had a Grand Master in Virginia who said let's do something. He appointed a Director of Education who agreed that something had to be done. They asked me to conduct weekend seminars in some areas of our state for those interested in leadership. This was done. We used motion pictures and other visual aids. We had those attending read a book on leadership before the seminar so we could get the participation we had to have. We started at 9 a.m. on Saturday and ended at noon on Sunday. The immediate results were great. I can truthfully claim that every man who attended those seminars went on to make top-notch Worshipful Masters. They knew there was more to Freemasonry than parroting the ritual.

Why weren't they continued into the next and following years? They were too successful! The questions asked of the top leadership by those attendees were too searching, too intelligent. There were other reasons, but all focused in the same direction.

Let there be light! Let us search for more and more light. With light comes truth; with truth comes growth; with growth comes an opportunity to continue to work for our God, our fellowman, our country, and the world. With this growth can also come Freemasonry's ultimate goal: the Brotherhood of Man throughout the world.

Stewart W. Miner, when he was Grand Master of Masons in Virginia, asked us to HOLD HIGH THE TORCH and let the light of Freemasonry blaze forth everywhere.

Isn't this worth working and fighting for?

Note: The television show mentioned was "The John Ankerberg Show" carried via cable and satellite. The "turncoat" mentioned was a Past Master of a Maryland Lodge. At the time this talk was presented, the producers of the show were attempting to have me appear on it. I told them I would provided it was broadcast live, or if they gave me editorial control. They wouldn't agree to that. But they also wouldn't take "NO" for an answer to my appearance. I sent them a portion of this paper, and suggested they read Matthew, Chapter 7, *"as there is a lot of Freemasonry there." I heard no more from them!*

What follows was presented at the Annual York Rite Assembly, commonly called "the Smokey Mountain Festival," at Waynesville, North Carolina, July 10, 1984. It was printed in the Royal Arch Mason, *Fall 1984.*

Freemasonry—Challenge of Tomorrow

Cervantes told us **"By the street of 'By and By' one arrives at the house of 'Never.'"**

That's an easy street to travel. It doesn't require any thought and certainly no action. By traveling on this street a fellow can remain popular. He won't disturb the *status quo*. He can't make anyone angry because he will propose nothing, which means he will do nothing. He'll also arrive with dispatch at the house of **"Never."**

I fear we've been traveling on the street of **"By and By"** in Freemasonry for far too many years. We've been content to sit on the Craft's laurels of the past. As a consequence we've fallen further and further behind man's progress in this Twentieth Century.

We've been far too content to put off until tomorrow, or next year, or the next decade, what we should have done yesterday. We just may have lost too many opportunities of the yesterdays gone by to catch up with tomorrow.

How often have you heard: "It can't be done!" in one form or another? This is one reason I place a copy of my favorite cartoon where everyone can see it when I conduct a seminar. Once you claim: "It can't be done!" there is one thing certain—it won't get done!

You're all familiar with this poem by Brother Edgar A. Guest, one of the early Fellows of The Philalethes Society:

Somebody said it couldn't be done,
But he with a chuckle replied
That "maybe it couldn't," but he would be one
Who wouldn't say so 'till he'd tried.
So, he buckled right in, with the trace of a grin
On his face. If he worried he hid it.
He started to sing as he tackled the thing
That couldn't be done, and he did it!

131

There's the greatest solution to the problems confronting us today. I couldn't resist offering this suggestion for solving many of our problems this early.

Take the "can't" out of Freemasonry's vocabulary along with the word "impossible" and you'll be surprised at the success you'll achieve. Sure you'll make mistakes. The only way not to err now and then is to travel on the street of By and By toward the house of Never.

With this sage advice I could quit here and we could all go home. But let me give you some of my thinking about where we're using "can't" and "impossible."

When we look at some of the problems confronting us today we must realize they didn't come upon us overnight. They started years ago and have grown out of all proportion, mainly because we've been traveling on the street of By and By. Like the mythical ostrich, we've been burying our heads in the sands of oblivion. We've been hoping if we didn't look, if we ignored them, they would go away. They haven't—and they won't—unless we stop sitting on our hands and get off the street of By and By.

Problem number one, if we are to believe the laments we hear and read constantly, is the loss of members.

Number two is the lack of attendance. Number three, poor leadership. Number four, little or no money. Five, poor ritual.

This list could be expanded *ad nauseam.* But if we can solve these five we'll get off the street of By and By leading toward the house of Never. We'll march briskly down the avenue of "Recovery." These are the "problems" we'll share as we accept the challenge to Freemasonry as we move into the last years of the Twentieth Century.

When we remove our heads from the sands of oblivion we'll recognize that each of these, and all other, problems are the result of poor leadership. I have another term for it that I'll not put into print. Although we'll be reluctant to admit it, the leaders of our Craft throughout the country, and the world, have been and are the culprits.

Freemasonry's challenge for tomorrow must begin today. Far too much time, manpower, and resources have been lost forever. We simply cannot lose any more—not if there is to be an organization called Freemasonry tomorrow.

Not too many months ago the now Grand Master of Masons in Pennsylvania, William A. Carpenter, and I were sharing many thoughts about Freemasonry. After hours of discussion we came to the same conclusion: **Unless there is a drastic change within the Craft there will be no recognizable Freemasonry within two decades.**

We are not referring to the Landmarks (whatever they are), the tenets or principles of Freemasonry. These do not need to be changed. We are referring to the thinking and actions of far too many men who know little or nothing about Masonry but who are placed in positions of leadership. We are referring to leaders who work for nothing but titles and self- glorification.

We are referring to those dubious leaders who surround themselves with men who know less than they do. This is one of the greatest mistakes any leader can make. This ensures the continuation of mediocrity. This is one error I've tried not to make. Often I've been complimented because each of my thirteen films has won an award in international competition. But I don't deserve the credit. I surround myself with a film crew that knows more than I'll ever know about cinematography, sound, lighting, editing and so on. They are paid well for their services so I expect the best productions possible within the capabilities of the budgets.

THERE CAN BE NO DEDICATION WITHOUT EDUCATION. I've said this over and over again. I'll continue stressing it. And I'll use my film crew as an example. Each is a specialist in his field. Each has studied, and continues to study, his specialty. Each compliments the whole. They know and enjoy what they do. They are dedicated because they are educated.

Why have many of you spent your lives working for the Craft? I think it's safe to claim you've done it because you are dedicated to the principles of Freemasonry. You've educated yourselves in this "profession." You had to do

133

it yourself because there was little, if any, help to be found anywhere. This is the foundation of our problems—the lack of education.

THERE IS NOTHING MORE EXPENSIVE THAN IGNORANCE. I've also made this claim many times before. We see the results of this ignorance every day, and not just in the Craft. When was the last time you walked into a store and received intelligent service? The "store" can be substituted for just about anything: business, profession, doctor's office, hospital.

Let's not go too far from "home." When was the last time you received an intelligent answer to some of your questions about Freemasonry?

The night before I left to come here I spoke in a local lodge. A young fellow came to me at the close of the meeting. He was concerned. He wanted to learn more about Freemasonry. He asked a high ranking ritualist how he could learn something about Masonry. This is the answer he received: "Read and inwardly digest, young man." Now that's a typical answer for a dyed-in-the-wool ritualist. He doesn't have to know anything himself. Let the other fellow do the reading and digesting. "Don't bother me, the ritualist." And if we inwardly digest we aren't sharing our knowledge and ideas with anyone. What good is knowledge if we don't share it?

You've heard many times the suggestion that we should reach out and touch someone. We're doing that all the time. But, unfortunately, the touch is too often negative. That's certainly not good for our Fraternity.

Many, many years ago I attempted what the networks have been doing in recent years—exit polling. I wanted to find out why good men were demitting from the Craft. Those who would talk about their reasons had many. But the predominate one was the desire to learn what Freemasonry is all about only to have their efforts ignored. I could empathize with them. I had the same problem over thirty-five years ago. That's why I've been pleading for our leadership to provide meaningful Masonic education.

So, we find that problem number one, the loss of members, is caused mainly by a lack of communication. This lack of communication is caused by a lack of knowledge. We don't know enough about Freemasonry to discuss it intelligently.

You have heard "there are no secrets in Freemasonry." **And there are no secrets.** Most good-sized book stores have books readily available for the public revealing everything there is to know about the Craft.

We can take comfort in our poor communication if we want to. The lack of communication is the number one problem in every business and organization. Frankly, I'm not comforted because there is no legitimate excuse for a lack of information anywhere. There is no excuse for a lack of training and little or no education.

An advertising blurb I recently received to try to induce me to attend a high-priced training conference stated: "The coming changes will force us to seek retraining again and again. Business will have to play the key role, similar to the way IBM now spends approximately $500 million annually on employee training and education."

Does this expenditure pay off for IBM? You can bet your tin whistle it does. Look at the way this "Johnny-come-lately" into the personal computer field has monopolized the market. Businesses consider a computer that isn't an IBM, or at least IBM compatible, not worth purchasing.

The same blurb reminds us that in business people must learn, unlearn and retrain constantly. This is true. You know it has been true in the past. It will be even more so tomorrow. The advertisement reminds us that audio/visual aides and computers will be needed to transmit education and skills to the individual. Another truism.

If it's true in business, why isn't it also true for fraternal organizations, especially Freemasonry?

Training and education are absolutely necessary if we are to attract good men into the Fraternity. They are a necessity if we are to keep them in our lodges, chapters, councils, and the commandery. We must train the leaders of today so they can educate those who will follow them tomorrow. This will take money, something too many of us are so reluctant to talk about we'd rather keep traveling on the street of By and By.

But didn't it disturb you yesterday morning when the moderator asked those over 65 to stand and 90% did. Then he asked those under 40 to stand. Two men stood! Two men out of this whole group! And there are those who think we're doing nothing wrong.

Unity

You are all familiar with the old clichés: "Divide and conquer"; "United we stand; divided we fall"; "for want of a nail a battle was lost"; and I like what Brother Benjamin Franklin said: "We must all hang together or assuredly we shall hang separately." We have been hanging separately; it's time we decided to hang together.

General Foch is quoted as saying during World War I: "My right has been rolled up. My left has been driven back. My center has been smashed. I have ordered an advance from all directions." And, by golly, out of the jaws of defeat he and his men achieved a great victory!

We are in a war today. It's a war of ideas; of morals; of brotherhood. It doesn't take much research to determine we're losing the battle. We're losing because we don't know why we're being defeated. We're hanging separately when we should be hanging together.

The four Masonic bodies represented here could "advance on all fronts" if they would work together. Instead they are diluting their manpower, resources, and time.

We find practically the same officers serving in each of these bodies, especially the chapter and council. Dues and contributions are paid to each body thereby spreading their meager resources too thin to do what is necessary. Time is used up by the few workers in constant meetings of these bodies. This causes attendance in each body to be low. There are just so

many hours in a day, just so many days in a week. Men must adopt priorities. Their families are going to insist on it.

Not your families and mine. They have given us their support as we work for Freemasonry. But there are three and a half million Masons in this country. Out of these there are only a handful like us. Think about it. What about the others?

There is a solution in part. What I've stated here has been recognized in many jurisdictions. Studies have been made that show the validity of what I've claimed. But, unfortunately, a choice was made to continue on the street of By and By. Heads went back into the sand to wait for the problems to disappear.

The solution? You know what it is. A few of you can see the logic in it. Others never will. It's to bring the Grand Councils into the Grand Chapters; to merge the General Grand Council with the General Grand Chapter. You don't believe it can be done? Think back to 1813 when the two rival Grand Lodges in England united.

Before you prepare the rope for the lynching let me give you my reasoning. I've already mentioned attendance. Under a merger this will improve somewhat, but not dramatically. It will take more than the coming together of the chapters and councils to do that. It will take imaginative and knowledgeable leadership to win back the defectors. But it will be a start.

It will be a start because one body instead of two will have more money to work with. Usually the dues for a chapter is much lower than they are for a lodge. This is as it should be. We must never forget where the foundation of Freemasonry is. For a council the rate is about half what it is for a chapter. If this was to go into one fund there could be more fellowship dinners, programs, and other festivities of interest to our members.

Fortunately we never have to worry about the ritualists. They will show up every time the doors open. But what about the 95% who are not interested in seeing the degrees performed over and over again? Should we continue to ignore them?

The General Grand Chapter is now receiving 15 cents per capita; so is the General Grand Council. Amazing! How in the world can service organizations be expected to provide substantial help with sums like those? Yet, even more amazingly, the General Grand Chapter through its Educational Bureau is doing a good job. We can thank a remarkable man, Charles K.A. McGaughey, for this and many other things. But remember, he can't continue forever.

Wouldn't it be better for the York Rite of Masonry if the chapters and councils merged and the per capita went into one service fund? They just might even come close to eventually obtaining a higher per capita. Most of you are Scottish Rite Masons. So am I. But I have long been disturbed by the great strides made by those two national bodies at the expense of Capitular Masonry. To me, nothing is more beautiful than the work of Royal Arch and Council degrees, when properly performed. Nothing is closer to Ancient Craft Masonry than is the Royal Arch. Yet nothing is sold cheaper. The Northern and Southern Jurisdictions of the Scottish Rite have millions of dollars invested; Capitular Masonry virtually nothing.

Why? Why has the Scottish Rite become the apex of Freemasonry? It wasn't always this way. Once York Rite Masonry was in the forefront. But for the past several years it has lost ground constantly, and it's continuing to lose out.

Could it be because the Scottish Rite advertises it holds the 33rd and last degree of Freemasonry? Could it be because its members can boast of being 32nd degree Masons, when in reality they are 32nd degree Scottish Rite members? Could it be because of its award system of red hats and white hats and that highly cherished 33rd degree?

What does the York Rite offer those who work in its quarries? The KYCH—but only to those who have presided over all *four York Rite Bodies*. This excludes thousands of Masons who deserve some reward for their efforts. These include men who for religious or other reasons cannot or choose not to belong to one of the three bodies that follow the Symbolic Lodge. There's no such criteria in the other Rite.

Isn't it long past time for the York Rite to recognize those of its workers who haven't "presided over all four York Rite Bodies?" Isn't it time to match, or surpass, the highly touted 32nd or the "33rd and last degree in Freemasonry?"

"We have awards," I can hear some of you say. True. The General Grand Chapter allows you to select one man each year to receive the Bronze Medal. It also awards a few Silver and Gold Medals every three years. I'm one of those fortunate few who holds the Silver. Some of the Grand Chapters and Councils reward one or two workers each year with medals. After years of needling Grand High Priests in Virginia I finally found one with courage enough to adopt an award of excellence. I suggested these go to three (a small number) each year. This was reduced to one.

We have a traveling degree team in Virginia that many of you are familiar with. It's now in its twenty-second year, which is remarkable when you consider degree teams usually function for six months or so. From the beginning we adopted a Virginia Craftsmen Distinguished Service Medal. We have no restrictions about how many or to whom they may be awarded. Some years we've presented as many as ten; other years, none. They go only to those who have *worked* for Freemasonry.

Unity is another answer as to why the Scottish Rite is more successful than the York Rite. And add money to the list. With all appendant bodies subordinate to the Supreme Councils, their control is complete. The per capita is established so that the Supreme Councils can hire the men they consider the best as their leaders. There is no skimping on money for salaries and expenses.

Do you think the Grand Commanders and their deputies spend a nickel of their own money traveling to promote the Scottish Rite? They don't. Now ask any Grand High Priest, Illustrious Grand Master, the General Grand High Priest and his deputies, along with the General Grand Secretary how much of their own money it costs them to hold their offices. I'll bet they can't tell you, because, like me, they're afraid to keep a record of how much it's costing them to serve the Craft.

Please don't misunderstand me. I'm not opposed to what the Scottish Rite has done and is doing. I want you to take some pages from their book.

Service

You all know I have no status whatsoever in the General Grand Chapter, never have had and never will. My Grand Chapter unfortunately doesn't belong to it. Even if it did I wouldn't be eligible to have a voice in it. But I respect what, through you, it is trying to do. It's trying to be a servant to York Rite Masonry in much the same way The Masonic Service Association is to the Grand Lodges. This isn't easy.

One of the best friends I'll ever have was Conrad Hahn. For over twenty years, while he was Executive Secretary of the MSA, we spent thousands of hours together. At his memorial service in 1977 several members of his staff told me he was closer to me than he was to any of them. The reason? He could "let his hair down" with me and know what he said in confidence would go no further. You would be amazed at how tight a line he had to walk to hold the voluntary association of Grand Lodges together.

Your General Grand Chapter officers have the same problem. Any of you can pull your Grand Chapter away. You know this. You recently watched two of the larger bodies walk out. You know there are others who won't join in your attempt to strengthen York Rite Masonry.

There's a great lesson here. The lack of unity today, and over the years, has weakened York Rite Masonry while the Scottish Rite, with its unity, has grown stronger. I'm not in a position to attempt to unify the York Rite, but many of you are. For the sake of all of us who love this Ancient Craft, I pray you will work together.

Unity will solve some of our problems. It will help with our attendance. It will conserve the energy of our officers. It will put our money into larger pots where it will do more good. It can help with our other problems— membership, leadership, and ritual.

Education—A Must

Conferences are being held constantly. What comes from them, however, is lost. Money being spent by Grand bodies and individuals to attend these sessions is too often wasted. This need not and should not be.

WITHOUT EDUCATION THERE CAN BE NO DEDICATION I said earlier. I can't emphasize this enough. Somewhere, somehow, York Rite Masonry in general and Freemasonry as a whole must find a way to coordinate that which is being lost. We must stop inventing the wheel over an over again. What comes out of each conference should be made available to everyone. There must be a clearing house for Masonic information.

Once there was something of this nature. We had Fraternal Correspondents, called by varying names, in every Grand body. Today there are only three or four of us left. Without this correspondence, this give and take over the years, I would never have been able to write some of the books I have. They kept us informed about what was going on in the Masonic world. They disseminated Masonic information. We need to bring them back.

We also need some full-time Masonic educators. I say full-time because it's difficult indeed to develop programs, train other educators, and also earn a living in another field. This, I know you're saying, "will cost money." Sure it will. But again I remind you THERE IS NOTHING MORE EXPENSIVE THAN IGNORANCE.

Would it be worth ten cents per member to do away with all our problems? To increase our membership thereby increasing the funds available; to drastically increase our attendance; improve our ritual; and provide excellent leadership way into the Twenty First Century? Through unity, without giving up any sovereignty, this can be accomplished.

The fund could be administered by the General Grand Chapter, or some central entity established by the leaders of York Rite Masonry. There would be money then to employ a top-notch *Masonic* educator, one who knows what Freemasonry is and should be. He could establish educational programs, develop leadership courses, and teach interested groups from each contributing jurisdiction. He could show us how to employ the modern tools now used everywhere but in Freemasonry for training.

This cannot be fully workable in a year, but a start would be made. It will take two or more years for the results to become apparent. But the results should prove highly dramatic. And because too many of our Grand Lodges are doing little or nothing to educate Master Masons, you will have a gold mine! I predicted many years ago that the appendant body that developed a good educational program for Freemasonry would grow rapidly. Master Masons are hungry for Masonic information and leadership training. I know because there is hardly a day that goes by that I don't receive a phone call or letter asking for help in some area of Freemasonry. No appendant body has accepted my challenge as yet. You have another opportunity to get off the street of By and By and work for the growth of York Rite Masonry.

In the meantime there is nothing to keep you from getting off this infamous street right now. You can set up your own "department of Masonic education." (Or call it what you will.) You've got men ready and willing to go to work. Every jurisdiction does. Many of these men have never been asked to help. When they are, they'll jump at the opportunity.

Keep your ritual strong. But stop making it the beginning and end of York Rite Masonry. Develop some good programs. Get back to the festive board. Put fun back into the Craft. Once you do you'll be amazed at the results.

Speculative Freemasonry didn't begin in 1717 as a solemn, puritanical fraternity. It began with a series of feasts. It continued around the festive board. When gentlemen of somber tastes gained control, the English Grand Lodge split in two in 1751. The one that continued its dreary ways lagged way behind the offshoot. There's another lesson there.

Recently one of you here today who is deeply concerned about the future of Freemasonry, especially Royal Arch Masonry, asked me some searching questions. One of them: "Why is leadership a 'no, no?' We want it but we don't want it. When we get some, we reject it." I touched on the answer earlier. Those of you who belong to The Philalethes Society will find a more comprehensive answer to that in the series on leadership I'm writing for its magazine.

Other questions he asked I'll try to answer briefly. "Why are there so few with knowledge of the Craft? Where are the students? If we lose them for more than a generation or two, won't Masonry become a mere social club, almost an opportunistic DooDoo bird?"

The answer to the last question is a resounding "Yes"!

The answers to his other questions are almost as easy. I've touched on them here. We have too few Masonically knowledgeable Masons because we have ignored Masonic education. Without an extensive knowledge of Freemasonry there can be few teachers. Without teachers there can be few students.

140

Without Masonic students, as I mentioned earlier, there will be no recognizable Freemasonry within two decades. There certainly is nothing more expensive than ignorance. It will destroy us. And I don't think you want that to happen.

If you have really listened to me up to this point, perhaps those of you with the power to do so will bring Masonry into the Twentieth Century. Then, and only then, we'll be in a position to develop the Masonic teachers, students and writers we must have to survive.

Twenty-two years ago I told the Northeast Conference on Masonic Education why we have few Masonic writers and authors. To put it simply it's because those who write for Freemasonry are expected to do it for free. It takes as long, if not longer, to research and write an article or book for Freemasonry than it does for the mass market. Those who are Masons and good writers aren't going to waste their time working for nothing. They've got to put bread on the table. (I don't know what catagory that puts me in.)

The same criteria holds true for Masonic speakers. They are expected to take hours preparing a speech, travel untold miles, take time away from gainful employment and give that speech before a sometimes appreciative audience of Freemasons, and pay their own expenses. Those same speakers could address civic clubs and other organizations and receive hundreds or thousands of dollars. Then they would even receive a note of thanks.

Conclusion

Let's bring unity to York Rite Masonry. You can do this even if you don't merge the Grand Chapters and Councils. But I think we will all be the beneficiaries if you do. Let's learn and teach the history, philosophy, symbolism, and brotherhood of the Craft. Let's stop trying to operate on pennies when we need dollars. Let's develop the constructive leaders we need for tomorrow.

Will this help put us on the avenue of Recovery? Will this bring a stronger Freemasonry into these latter years of the Twentieth Century? I think it will—**if you want it to.**

A wise old man lived in the mountains alone. People below said he knew the answers to everything. Three young men decided to fool him. One of them captured a bird and said to his friends: "Let's get the old man. No matter what he says, I'll prove he's wrong."

They climbed to the top of the mountain and reached the old man. The fellow with the bird said: "Wise old man, what have I in my hands?" A feather sticking out of the fellow's hand told the old man what he held. "A bird," he replied. The young fellow grinned: "Is it alive or dead?"

The old man knew what would happen when he answered. If he said it was dead, the young fellow would open his hands and let the bird fly away. If he said it was alive, the fellow would crush it and let it fall to the ground. So, looking the young man in the eye, he said: "As you will it, my son. As you will it."

141

Can Freemasonry meet the challenge of tomorrow?

What the wise old man said is our answer: **"As you will it. As you will it, my friends."**

[During the question and answer period I was asked why I had so obviously not included the Commandery in my suggestion for merger. I said I would be happy to, if the Commandery would change so Masons other than Christians could become members. Ancient Craft Masonry, at least since 1717, has been nondenominational. The Commandery is a Christian association of Masons, thereby excluding other religions. It has also been reported that the Grand Encampment will in no way approve a consolidation of the "three York Rite Bodies" unless it can be head of the body.]

After it was printed in the *Royal Arch Mason* a Companion took the editor and me to task because of my answer to the above. He ignored the article and concentrated only on the answer to the question. Unfortunately, I must stand by the answer I gave. Nothing has happened or been said since its publication to cause me to change my thinking. In fact, it has been strengthened.

Iowa Research Lodge No. 2 held a ladies night banquet in December 1985. Although it doesn't speak of leadership as such, it tells what Masonic leadership is. It depicts Masonic leadership in action. Although I didn't read this "script," it's basically what I said.

The Mystic Tie

Preamble

I have been led to believe that this part of the program is not supposed to be intellectual, so your program chairman certainly made an excellent choice.

Sometimes we get overly impressed with ourselves, especially when we get a title of some description. And, by golly, we've got plenty of titles in Freemasonry. In fact, we've got so many none of us know what they mean. In the business world it has become almost as bad. When a fellow, or lady, reaches his level of incompetency he usually becomes a vice president.

A couple of fellows were talking the other day about how important they were. One of them, a vice president, got downright obnoxious, so his friend decided to put him in his place. "Joe," says he, "vice presidents are a dime a dozen."

"That's not so," said Joe indignantly. "You've got to have something on the ball to reach that high level in any business."

"I'll prove you're wrong," said his friend. He picked up the phone and called a local supermarket. "Let me talk to the vice president in charge of prunes." The voice on the other end asked: "Packaged or bulk?"

Two fellows were sharing a room in an old Baptist hospital. With nothing to do they became bored and decided to play poker. When they asked the nurse for playing cards, her frown could have frozen Hades. She relented, however, and brought them a flock of cards containing case histories. The fellows agreed these were better than nothing, so one shuffled and dealt them.

The first fellow said: "I've got two appendectomies and two tonsillectomies." The other said: "I've got four enemas."

"Then," said the first fellow, "you take the pot. You need it more than I do."

A right good minister always used a manuscript when he preached his sermons. A member of his flock decided one Sunday morning to have a little fun with him, so he took the last two pages of his manuscript out of his notebook. The preacher got along fine. He was preaching up a storm. Everyone could tell he was reaching the climax when he shouted: "And Adam said to Eve; and Adam said to Eve; and Adam said to Eve," and almost in a whisper: "There seems to be a leaf missing."

Let's get serious for a few moments.

What is this tie that binds most Freemasons together? What is it that makes the heart beat a little faster when a Brother receives an honor or achieves a great victory? What is it that makes a Brother weep with another in his sorrow, and makes one go out of his way to help the distressed?

What tie is it that unites the families of Brothers, and makes the happiness and problems of each their own?

Think along with me for a few moments and let us try to find the answer. As we consider the questions let's look at some who may have found the answer.

One of these Freemasons was Joseph Fort Newton. In his autobiography, *River of Years*, Brother Newton tells us his father was made a Freemason in a Military Lodge. During the course of a battle his dad, a Confederate was captured by Union troops. He was subsequently taken to a prison camp at Rock Island, Illinois. While there he became deathly ill, but he managed to make himself known as a Mason.

A Federal officer, a Freemason, took him to his home, nursed him back to health and when the war was over, gave him money and a gun so Newton could return to his home to Texas.

Joseph Newton, the son, was so impressed by this act, which he said made the hells of war more endurable and the Fraternity that could remember a Brother's welfare in times like those, that he petitioned a Lodge as soon as he was old enough to do so. That eminent Mason and minister enriched the literature of Freemasonry with several books and hundreds of talks, articles and sermons.

During a particularly stormy session of a meeting of The Masonic Service Association, when Brothers were fighting Brothers and Grand Lodges quitting the Association, Newton told those present:

"Freemasonry's simplicity, its dignity, and its spirituality sustain me in all that I try to do, and permit me to forget the incredible pettiness of mind that we sometimes encounter, sustaining and enabling me to join hands with my Brethren everywhere, to do something, if it be only a little, before the end of the day, to make a gentler, kinder, and wiser world in which to live."

I have never found another writer who could so easily turn prose into beautiful poetry. Newton was convinced, and so am I, that Freemasonry is that answer to most of the problems found in the world today. I should qualify this statement—the principles of Freemasonry are the answer.

This was another of those cases that proves Brotherly Love has no stopping point. Just a little goes far and endures from age to age.

Among the many others who found this tie was Henry Price of Massachusetts, who almost single-handed kept Freemasonry alive in the formative years beginning in 1733. Then there was another Massachusetts Mason, Melvin Maynard Johnson, who early in the Twentieth Century worked for all branches of Masonry. His writings were monumental; his research extraordinary (even though he attempted to make Massachusetts Masonry first in everything). His speeches and articles on Masonic law and the rights of Grand Lodges over all other bodies kept the Masonic hierarchy on a straight path.

George Washington definitely found this tie. He spent his lifetime working for his colony of Virginia. He was indispensable to the people of the new United States of America in war and in peace. These activities kept him from being an active participant in Masonic Lodges, but didn't diminish his love for the Craft. He supported it whenever possible.

Benjamin Franklin was one of the few businessmen who worked for the freedom of America without seeking a profit. No job was too small or unimportant for him to tackle for his country. He was one of the first men to recognize the importance of Freemasonry in the colonies of the New World. He was active in Masonic affairs here and in France throughout his life. He was another who found this tie we're trying to define.

Newton's was one example of this peculiar tie at work during the War Between the States. Another example occurred in the village of Hampton, Virginia. It was about to be burned by Union Forces. When the commanding officer learned there was a Masonic Lodge in the town, he sent some of his men into the temple to remove the jewels, charter and records. Then he ordered every building in the town burned to the ground, including the Masonic hall.

The objects removed from the Lodge were sent to the Grand Lodge of Maryland with the request that they be turned over to the Grand Lodge of Virginia as soon as possible. This was done before the war had ended.

Early in 1864 Federal troops took over Winchester and held it until well after hostilities had seized. Earlier, when the Federals had occupied Winchester they had permitted Winchester-Hiram Lodge No. 21 to operate, and several Union officers and men had received their degrees there. Because of that a committee from the Lodge attempted to see General Sheridan, the Commanding Officer, but he refused to interview them, until one of the officers of the Lodge contacted a friend in the cabinet in Washington. The resulting note speedily gave them an audience with Sheridan.

Sheridan refused to let the Lodge reopen, as had been expected, because of his religious and political views. But one of his staff officers, a Mason, argued in favor of the Lodge. He promised to be in attendance at all its meetings and report to the commander anything detrimental to the Union cause. Sheridan finally reluctantly agreed.

As a result of the resumption of labor, 207 members of the Federal troops were made Master Masons in that Lodge. Among them was a Captain from Ohio, William McKinley, who was later to become President of the United States and fall from an assassin's bullet. Several men later awarded the Congressional Medal of Honor were also among them.

Picture, if you will, those Confederate Masons making Masons of those who captured their town a short time earlier. Where can we find a more graphic picture of the Universality of Masonry? When political enemies can lay aside their differences to meet on the level and part upon the square, Freemasonry has something the whole world needs.

I want to add this footnote: during this "brothers' war," except from one Grand Master, not a single word was uttered that could be termed unMasonic. Nor as far as I can determine, was a Freemason, even though on the opposite side, refused help from another Mason. When you think of the period, that was remarkable!

The year was 1863. New Orleans had fallen before Farragut's fleet and Butler's army. Up and down the Mississippi river ranged Union gunboats. Among them was the United States steamer *Albatross,* with Lieutenant-Commander John E. Hart, United States Navy, of Schenectady, New York, and a member of St. George's Lodge No. 6, Free and Accepted Masons, as her commander. Captain Hart was stricken with a fever contracted on duty that held him, delirious, in his bunk in his tiny stateroom.

In the log of the *Albatross,* the following official entry yet survives in the navy department archives at Washington: "June 11, 1863: 4:15 p.m. The report of a pistol was heard in the captain's stateroom. The steward at once ran in and found the captain lying on the floor with blood oozing from his head and a pistol near him, one barrel of which was discharged. The surgeon was at once called but life was extinct."

On Captain Hart's personal official record in the navy department archives is the charitable notation, "Died of wounds," although there is no doubt that, in his delirium, he shot himself.

There was no Confederate force at St. Francisville that day to defend the town. The lovely old place lay passive and took 108 shells, which riddled the old courthouse, ruined Grace church, and shattered the beautiful stained-glass window above the altar. The few Confederate soldiers there on leave could only grind their teeth in impotent rage.

Suddenly, the firing ceased. Those who watched from the bluff saw a ship's boat put out from the *Albatross,* an officer in the stern, Union sailors rowing, and in the bow a white flag.

Two brothers dwelt at the foot of the bluff, Samuel and Benjamin White, both of them Masons. They met the Union naval officer as the boat docked. The officer asked: "Is there a Mason in this town?"

They told him there was. The officer told them to inform the Master they had the body of a Mason who had requested a Masonic funeral ashore before he had died. The Master of the Lodge was with the Confederate forces in another State, but W. W. Leake, the Senior Warden was in town on furlough. When informed of the situation, he said: "It is my duty as a Mason to set aside politics and do what I can for a Brother Mason." He agreed to conduct the funeral.

The flag of truce yet flying, the men from the *Albatross* carried Captain Hart's body ashore, clad in the uniform of a United States naval officer. At the foot of the bluff to meet it, their Masonic regalia worn above their uniforms of Confederate gray, stood four members of Feliciana Lodge No. 31 of St. Francisville. Among them were two brothers, Samuel and Benjamin White. The Masons of the *U. S. S. Albatross* identified themselves to the Masons of the Confederate army.

Up the bluff and into the little white wooden home of Feliciana Lodge No. 31, that still stands, but is a public library now, they bore the body. Over it they conducted the ancient funeral service of Masonry. Then to the cemetery in the churchyard of Grace Church, pitted with the shell holes from that dead officer's own guns, they went to the grave St. Francisville's Masons had dug. With Masonic ritual, they consigned all that was mortal of Lieutenant-Commander John E. Hart, United States Navy.

When the newly turned earth lay above the coffin the shore party of the *Albatross* saluted and departed for their gunboat, unmolested. The watching Confederates on the top of the bluff, amid the shell-shattered wreckage of what had been beautiful St. Francisville, saw the *Albatross* up-anchor, swing around and steam down the Mississippi river.

But that was not the end of this picture of Brotherly Love. Throughout the years the Masons of St. Francisville, and the Daughters of the Confederacy, kept that grave green and fresh, along with those of the Southerners. In 1956 the Grand Lodge of Louisiana erected a monument over that grave replacing the simple head-stone that marked Brother Hart's last resting place.

To commemorate this historical event, the Grand Lodge of Louisiana invited the Virginia Craftsmen to its jurisdiction and St. Francisville. There, with appropriate ceremonies, a memorial service was held at the grave of John E. Hart on October 2, 1972. A wreath was laid at the head of the monument that covered the entire length of Hart's grave.

Found in the inscription of that monument are the words with which this story ends: "This monument is dedicated in loving tribute to the Universality of Freemasonry."

Many Masons have found the beauty of this tie that appears to be peculiar to those who have learned the teachings of Freemasonry.

Let's go back three decades to the years of the anti-Masonic craze that started in 1826 and was particularly violent in the 1830s. This began with the supposed "murder" of one William Morgan. The anti-Masons used what was not a murder but a disappearance to crucify the Craft. They almost succeeded.

This wasn't the first attack on the Craft, nor will it be the last. It's prevalent today and getting more vicious all the time. These attacks were first recorded in 287 A.D. when four Masons were put to death by Diocletian. Their crime? They refused to build a pagan statue! Their fortitude has been commemorated by Quatuor Coronati Lodge, the London Lodge of Research.

After the formation of the Grand Lodge of England in 1717 attacks became more vocal and the press then, as now, made more of them than they rated.

Even though these attacks continued, none were more disastrous than those of the 1830s in this country. It was particularly horrible in the East where hundreds of Lodges gave up their charters and thousands of Masons quit. Many of them renounced Freemasonry so they could take communion in their churches.

It was only in those states, Massachusetts, Connecticut, and Rhode Island, where Masonry fought back that the critics were whipped. To its credit, not a single Lodge in Rhode Island gave up its charter, but every Lodge in Vermont did. When Pennsylvania decided not to "turn the other cheek" any longer and fight, the craze quickly ended.

There were a few during that trying time who knew what this tie we're discussing was. One in particular was the Reverend George Taft, D.D., Minister of the First Baptist Church in the little village of Pawtucket, Rhode Island. Here's what the Grand Master of 1869 said of him:

Throughout the dark days of Anti-Masonry in R.I. he traveled throughout his state to conduct Masonic funerals—braving the jeers and stones of the anti-Masons. He died on December 11, 1869, at the age of 78. The day he was carried to his grave, every business in the village of Pawtucket was closed, his church wouldn't hold all who wanted to attend his funeral. As his body was carried to the grave the bells of all the churches tolled his requiem, people all along the route openly wept.

The principles of a good man, a proud Master Mason, a devoted man of God, had proven stronger than the seeds of hate cast by unprincipled "clergymen" and politicians.

Then there was Andrew Jackson, a Past Grand Master of Masons in Tennessee, who refused to renounce Freemasonry although he was running for the Presidency. He was elected and re-elected, proving again a man with principles will outlast the demagogues. Another man who had found this mysterious tie in Freemasonry.

Let's skip a century to Harry S. Truman, the foremost Master Mason of the Twentieth Century. It has taken a book to tell the Masonic story of Brother Truman, a Past Grand Master of Masons in Missouri.

His story is typical of those who have found this beautiful "tie" in Freemasonry. It tells of hate, envy, jealousy, but underlying this—a tremendous love. He spent his life working for the people of America—and Freemasonry

You don't have to be a Mason to find this tie we've been discussing. Without question, Sam Walter Foss knew what it was. Listen again to these words:

Let me live in my house by the side of the road,
Where the race of men go by—

They are good, they are bad, they are weak, they are strong.
Wise, foolish—so am I;
Then why should I sit in the scorner's seat,
Or hurl the cynic's ban?
Let me live in my house by the side of the road,
And be a friend to man.

Listen again to the words of a man who may have been a Mason, St. Francis of Assisi:

"Lord, make me an instrument of your peace; where there is hatred, let me sow love; where there is injury, pardon; where there is doubt, faith; where there is despair, hope; where there is darkness, light; and where there is sadness, joy. O Divine Master, grant that I may not so much seek to be consoled as to console; to be understood as to understand; to be loved as to love; for it is in giving we receive, it is in pardoning that we are pardoned, and it is in dying that we are born to eternal life. Amen."

This peculiar tie has been called "The Mystic Tie." Perhaps rightly so. What is it? Only your heart can give you the answer.

Potpourri

Tips for writers doesn't pretend to be all-inclusive, nor is it what all editors are looking for. Every worthwhile publication has its own rules, usually called a manual of style. Before writing something for a particular periodical, study several issues. This will help you learn what the editors want.

A couple of years ago while attending the Allied Masonic meetings in D.C., a fellow asked what it took to be a writer. I told him I was still trying to find out myself. But I suggested the first thing a writer had to do was read, read, read. "Oh, I don't read," he said. "I hate it. But I know I'd be a good writer." I left it at that.

Tips for Writers

When writing for publications little things are important. Editors, whether they are with newspapers or magazines, can tell quickly whether or not to read what you've sent. While we don't have the space for a course in writing, we believe these tips will prove helpful.

- Never, never send an editor a handwritten manuscript. That makes them shudder. Almost without exception your masterpiece will be promptly consigned to the wastebasket.
- Always use a typewriter with **clean keys.** Make certain the ribbon produces clear copy. Faded ribbons and dirt-clogged keys produce manuscripts difficult to read and impossible to photocopy. Don't start with two strikes against you.
- Double space your copy on cheap white bond paper. Don't use colored stock or "erasable" bond. The first might be hard to read; the second will smudge when handled by the editor, printer and others who have to work with it.
- Make your final rewrite as free of errors as possible. A few corrections in spelling and typos are understandable, but not wholesale changes. You've got to leave room for the editor's blue pencil (I use green).
- Put your name, address, and phone number on your manuscript or query—not just on the envelope. Envelopes have a way of disappearing in the trash.
- If you use initials, at least let the editor know if you're a Mr., Miss, Mrs. or Ms. He'll appreciate knowing how to address you and

get a perspective on your point of view, because sexes do have different viewpoints.

- Send your manuscript flat if it's more than four pages. Don't take a chance of losing part of it in an envelope slicer. Always enclose a self-addressed envelope with sufficient return postage (SASE).
- Pictures should always be protected from possible damage. Include suggested captions and correctly spelled names. They should be black and white glossies at least 5x7 unless otherwise specified by the publication.
- Watch your spelling! (I wear out dictionaries by the dozen—almost.) Let someone else do your proof reading. I do. One of my good friends tells me (truthfully) I've developed many "Robertseses"—these are words I think are spelled correctly, but they ain't.
- Punctuation and grammar are important, indeed. A misplaced comma can come back to haunt you. How about this for an example? "Before leaving the girls, clean up the office"—"Before leaving, the girls clean up the office." Who's going to clean up the office—you or the girls? The comma makes the difference.

Let's talk about some **Ground Rules** to use to make our writing interesting reading.

- Use contractions as often as possible. Words like "it's" or "doesn't" may sound trivial in trying to improve your writing style but there's nothing that's more important. You should try to write as you talk. By using contractions, you'll be doing just that.
- Leave out **that** whenever possible. Since **that** is one of the most frequently used words in the English language, there's an opportunity to eliminate the word in almost every paragraph you write. Leave it out whenever it sounds right to drop it. Your writing will be more fluent, more like "spoken" sentences. **Which** is another word to leave out of your writing as much as possible. But, if you have a choice between the two, use **that** rather than **which**.
- Use direct questions. Direct questions are an essential part of the spoken language. You can't conduct a true conversation without questions (except rarely). Even in your writing there's plenty of opportunity to express what is **actually** a question in the form of a **grammatical** question with a question mark at the end. Don't you agree?
- Use personal pronouns such as I, we, you, and they as much as possible. A speaker uses personal pronouns, doesn't he? (**See Tips for Speakers.**) Shouldn't you do the same in your writing?
- If possible, put prepositions at the end of a sentence. A preposition is a good word to end the sentence with (in spite of what you've been taught). And grammatical superstitions are something to get rid of. When Winston Churchill was chided for ending a sentence with a preposition, he told the chider: "Changing my writing is a practice up with which I will not put!"

- When you refer back to a noun or pronoun, repeat the noun or pronoun. Don't use some form of "elegant variation."
- Don't refer to what you **wrote** or are going to **write,** but to what you **talked about.** Don't use such words as **above, below** or **hereafter;** instead, say **earlier, later, from now on.** Don't turn every piece of writing into a fake antique.

I'd like to suggest you get a copy of **Say What You Mean** by Rudolf Flesch. He tells you how to do just that—say what you mean. The academic perfectionists won't agree with him, but you ain't going to be writing for them. There aren't many of them, but there sure are a lot of people like us who need to learn. And we want to enjoy what we read while we're learning. Don't we?

Now we'll discuss some tools every writer should have.

Every profession and trade must have its tools. Those of us who putter around the house soon learn we don't have the tools needed for most of the jobs to be done. Neither does the auto mechanic, the plumber, the electrician, or anyone else. They have the basic implements, but there are times when something not in the tool box is needed.

It's the same with the writer. He will never have all the tools he needs to do many jobs. My library consists of over 3,000 books, yet far too often I must refer to something I don't have, to write the article or book or script I'm working on. So, here we'll list the basic tools you'll need if you want to write.

First, a typewriter is almost a must. I would conservatively estimate you can type 25 times faster than you can write in longhand; about 35 times faster than you can print. There's a way out for the non-typist. He can use a tape recorder and have his words transcribed. Most businessmen do. Then, too, a tape recorder is a valuable tool for interviews.

Among the books you'll find essential are: A good **dictionary;** a **thesaurus;** an **atlas;** an **almanac; encyclopedia;** an **English grammar reference;** a **manual of style; general reference;** and on and on.

A good dictionary is absolutely necessary. Even top-notch spellers (and I'm certainly not one of them) don't know how to spell every word in use today. There are many excellent dictionaries available everywhere.

A thesaurus is termed "a treasury of words." It's better known as a book of synonyms, sometimes coupled with antonyms. Often we'll want to use two words with the same meaning in a paragraph to hold down repetition, or for some other reason. Such a book can prove invaluable, even if it isn't used often.

An atlas helps us to pinpoint locations. An almanac, literally concerns itself with days, months, and the year, but is generally considered to be a "year book." There are many good ones published each year. One of them can save you hours in researching a particular event.

Encyclopedias can also save hours. They just might have what you're looking for at a given time. While a few dictionaries will help with grammar, most won't. Almost everyone has forgotten (if they ever learned) the hundreds of rules of grammar taught in school. Here we won't argue if this is good or bad, but we must follow some guidelines or there will be chaos.

A manual of style gives us the road map we must have in writing. I have always used the one published by the University of Chicago. I mention this so you will know why quotation marks, with rare exceptions, are always placed outside of commas and periods in my writing. I shudder when I see them otherwise! It also will explain a few other things you find in what I write that differ from other publications. Every publisher of books, newspapers, magazines, and so on, has a style book that must be followed. So should you, even though minor changes will be made by the editor of the publication you write for.

General reference books will include anything and everything. Biographies, histories, "how to," catalogs, fiction, non-fiction, and whatever you have on your library shelves will all be used as reference material sometime. For specialized fields you will require specialized reference material. You can't write about medicine without having plenty of material in the field. You can't write for or about Freemasonry without an extensive library of Masonic material.

For Freemasonry (and that's what we're concerned with here) the reference books needed are without number. Here are some I consider necessary:

Coil's Masonic Encyclopedia is the most up-to-date general reference book on Freemasonry. It has out-dated Mackey's. It is as complete a history of the Craft as can be found in any one volume. For biographies, **10,000 Famous Freemasons,** compiled by William R. Denslow, is invaluable. After being out-of-print for years, it is again available in soft cover from the Royal Arch Educational Bureau. Hopefully, some enterprising writer will add another volume to cover the Freemasons who have become famous since 1961.

For leadership, **Key to Freemasonry's Growth** is still the only book on the subject addressed to the Craft. **The Craft and Its Symbols** cover this subject. Unfortunately, there is yet to be written a good book on Masonic jurisprudence.

This list can go on indefinitely. As with all articles, it must be "abandoned" somewhere. This is the place.

POSTSCRIPT FOR TIPS FOR WRITERS

Those of us who write have been blessed. Thanks to a small group of computer hackers who never believed the phrase "It Can't Be Done!"

Computers have been around for years. Until the '80s one had to have millions, if not billions of dollars to even look at one. They surely weren't accessible to those of us who write for Freemasonry. These hackers came to our rescue. They made computers available to us common folks. Today (1987) computers as powerful as those that once filled large, specially equipped rooms, sit on our desks.

Every month prices of computers are being reduced. Amazingly, along with the reduction in price there is an increase in power. Less than a decade ago high-priced computer programmers were needed to develop the simplest process to make those expensive machines work. Today thousands of inexpensive programs are available for every conceivable application.

Every lodge, Grand Lodge, and appendant body should now have all their records computerized. The miracle of the computer revolution has made record keeping available to all of us. The leadership that doesn't recognize this is OBSTRUCTIVE, indeed.

It would take volumes to cover the uses to which computers should be employed. It would take more volumes to record the history of the development of this remarkable creation. Here we must confine are remarks to the writer. Even so, what is covered must be far too short. Must books and magazines about computers will help fill in the blanks.

In 1982, after months of research on computers, I determined to purchase one. For varying reasons I decided I needed two disks drives, and this proved correct. With the announcement of the Osborne I, I concluded it was just what I needed. It not only had two disk drives, it had hundreds of dollars worth of software included. One of these was *WordStar* from MicoPro, a program for writers. It also had a CP/M system, for which hundreds of hackers had compiled public domain programs.

At that time I was writing *Freemasonry in American History,* so I switched from my trusty typewriter to the Osborne. The frustration started immediately. I had purchased, at full retail, the machine from the largest chain of computer stores in the country. They offered absolutely no help. It was almost a year before a Users' Group was formed. I was on my own.

Today, and four computers later, this is no longer the case. Computer users can find plenty of help. We don't have to depend on stores that offer high prices but no after-sales assistance. Excellent mail order houses with reasonable prices are available everywhere.

Now I use a PC AT with a 30mg hard disk and two floppy drives. The old *WordStar* has been greatly improved to version 4.0, and another update will be available shortly. Included with this program is a Thesaurus and a Dictionary. Gone are the tedious hours of proof reading to check the spelling. However, an "and" shows up as correct when we mean to use "an," so the human eye is still a necessity.

There are many other good word processing software programs. There are other programs to aid the writer. These will be found advertised in any good computer magazine. Every writer should obtain what he's comfortable with.

In "tips" I strongly suggested handwritten manuscripts should never be sent to an editor. With the computer age has come dot matrix printers. Many editors treat manuscripts printed with these as they do handwritten epistles.

Don't gamble. If you don't own a letter quality printer, take your disk to a friend or store where it can be printed properly.

All the "tips" preceding this Postscript are still important and necessary. The computer has simply made our work much easier.

Happy writing.

Here are a few tips for speakers. You'll have many you can add to the list. One I didn't mention, for instance, is breathing. I find if I take several deep breaths before starting to speak, it helps considerably. Then, too, it takes the audience a moment or two to get used to your voice. So I try to say something that means nothing for the first sentence or two. It gives the listeners an opportunity to settle in their seats and begin to look attentive.

There are no two speaking styles the same. That's good. Develop your own.

You'll note I've suggested you stay away from "dirty words." Conrad Hahn noted: "What are 'dirty words?' Depends on speaker and listener, no?" He's correct, of course. I have a good friend, a Past Grand Master, who can say most anything and have the audience rolling in the aisles. Often when he is introduced he'll suggest the audience take a "pee break" so they can listen to him undisturbed. Many take him up on it, laughing all the way to the "necessary." I know of only one or two others who could warm up the folks that way.

In the final analysis, you've got to be your own judge. As a rule I'm a "serious" talker. Rarely do I try to tell any jokes (although I've got plenty). But, occasionally, for programs where the ladies are present, I'll lighten up the dialogue. I did this for one group and have never had an audience laugh so heartily. Figured I had it made. A month or so later I gave the same talk before another group. It bombed!! I don't think I've ever been as embarrassed as I was that evening. So, find out who's going to be out front before you prepare anything to present.

Tips for Speakers

"Doesn't that guy have enough sense to shut up?" "He's rambling all over the place. Why can't he stick to one subject so I'll know what he's talking about?" "He kept saying 'You know.' If I had known I wouldn't have had to listen to him, would I?"

You can elaborate on these statements at length. Everyone of us has heard dozens of speeches in our Lodges. We've heard hundreds via radio or television. It's particularly bad during election years. That's when we learn what "double-talk" really is. We've all been annoyed by speakers who obviously didn't know their subject. Here are some tips to help you become an acceptable speaker, or help others who may be having problems.

- Be at ease. ALL speakers (who care) are nervous before they begin their speech. So don't feel you are alone. The professional speaker appears to be at ease, but he isn't. His experience before many audiences, however,

159

helps him to overcome his initial fear quickly; usually as soon as he begins to speak.

- Be well prepared. This will aid you in overcoming your initial fear. Start this preparation well in advance of your engagement. A week in advance may be sufficient, but, depending on the depth of the subject, it might takes months of research. Whatever it takes, take it.
- Be friendly. Your audience is on your side; it's really not composed of monsters. Look around. Pick out the most friendly faces and talk to them. Just make sure they're not on the same side of the room—or on the ceiling.
- Be a leader. Stand tall. Talk eye-to-eye with your audience. Speak with authority. Be positive, but friendly and straightforward at the same time.
- DON'T READ YOUR SPEECH. Use notes, if you must, but don't read. Few things are more boring than a reader who's supposed to be a speaker. You can't look your audience in the eye if your eyes are on a piece of paper.
- Keep your head. Don't become a zealot. Be confident but not overly so. Don't become intoxicated with a sense of your power. Keep your sense of humor.
- Be yourself. Say what YOU think, not what someone else thinks. Study other speakers, but don't imitate them. Develop your own style. Learn what makes YOU an effective speaker.
- Stay away from "dirty" words. There are a few (but just a few) speakers who can say almost anything and get away with it. The chances are you aren't one of them. So don't risk offending your audience. Many people are "broad-minded" but there are always some who aren't. Why gamble if you don't have to?
- Use personal pronouns. Why not say, "I'm happy to be with you this evening" rather than the drab, "You have made your speaker happy by inviting him to address you this evening"? "The speaker believes," will make your audience ask why YOU don't believe what you're saying.
- Learn to accept criticism. You will profit by it. Ask those you trust to analyze your performance. Discover your weaknesses; overcome them; don't continue to cover them up. Discover your strengths, then emphasize these strengths and develop them.

*Since 1918 The Masonic Service Association of the United States has been provid-
ing Freemasons and Grand Lodges with educational material. It's available to you for
the asking. There's hardly a Masonic topic that hasn't been covered. So, there's no
reason why you can't fulfill any engagement you may be requested to accept. If you
aren't good at research, it has been done for you.*
It is truly "Freemasonry's Servant." Use it.

Freemasonry's Servant

"Throughout the writing of this history one thought has persisted and has
not gone away," I wrote in 1969. "Would not Freemasonry in this country be
even better if all Grand Lodges had belonged to The Masonic Service Association and every Masonic leader had received the publications of the Association? Would not some of our governmental officers who are Masons have a
better concept of what a true republic is?"

This was in the preface of **Freemasonry's Servant,** the first 50 years of the
M.S.A. I believed then the answer was a resounding YES; I believe it even
more today. This is one organization that can speak as one voice for all of
Freemasonry—if our Grand Lodges will let it.

Let's look at the background of the M.S.A. briefly.

It was born in 1918, at the close of World War I. Why? Because the several
Grand Lodges and appendant bodies found the federal government wouldn't
deal with 49 plus enities. While other organizations were permitted to go
overseas to help our servicemen, Freemasonry couldn't. But what a difference just prior to and during World War II! Freemasonry, through the
M.S.A., spoke with a single voice.

A group of far-sighted and dedicated Masonic leaders formed the Association in Iowa in 1918. They spent days producing a constitution and by-laws
that any Grand Lodge could live with. It prohibited for all time the possibility
of this Association becoming the dreaded thing each Grand Lodge feared—a
General Grand Lodge. It was to be a voluntary organization composed of
Grand Lodges who voluntarily joined. A few Grand Lodges never have
joined; others joined and dropped out; many of the "dropouts" thankfully
returned.

161

During its almost 60 years, the M.S.A. has provided much needed educational material for Freemasons. It has acted as a Masonic collection agency for the victims of disasters. And nothing has ever been "taken off the top" for expenses. It has been able to protect the interests of the Craft when governmental policies could have created havoc.

"The necessity for a qualified Freemason to lead the Association was recognized at the organizational meeting," I wrote in the Epilogue. "The search was begun for a man with the personality of a matinee idol, the wisdom of Solomon, and the oratorical ability of a Cicero or a Demosthenes. The 'perfect' man was not found; he never will be, no matter how diligent the search."

Unfortunately the M.S.A. has been unable to accomplish all it should. It has operated on pennies when dollars are needed. It never has had the support of all the Grand Lodges in the United States. But, to the credit of many of these non-members, they did help during World War II to provide servicemen and women with "homes away from home." But why, why should it take adversity to bring a semblance of unity to Freemasonry?

Just so there will be no chance of you thinking I'm on the "payroll" of the M.S.A., I'm not and never have been. There are many things I've done for it. There are many things I hope to do for it in the future. Why? Not because I'll make any money (in fact, it has cost me money), but because it's endeavoring to help all Freemasons through their Grand Lodges.

Let me urge you to do two things, even if your Grand Lodge doesn't belong to The Masonic Service Association: Get the award-winning film "The Brotherhood of Man. . . ." and show it in your Lodge, or for an open program; Get a copy of **Freemasonry's Servant.** Both can be obtained from The Masonic Service Association, 8120 Fenton St., Silver Spring, MD 29010.

You'll find, as I have, that Freemasonry needs its Servant more than ever.

NOTE: The M.S.A. has another award-winning film now. It's "Fraternally Yours" and is ten minutes long, 16mm, color. It also has a wealth of **Short Talks** on hundreds of subjects, and other educational material. Write the M.S.A. for catalogs.

For the most part the editorials that appeared in The Altar Light *have not been reproduced here. What follows is an exception. The questions asked are pertinent to Masonic education and Masonic leadership.*

I didn't go into as much detail as perhaps I should have about placing Masonic educators on the same level as Masonic ritualists. It's a touchy subject. While only five percent of our members are ritualists, or interested in the ritual, they control the whole Fraternity. The lecture I gave a couple of years ago, and which Jerry wanted to include here, goes into more detail.

Until our Masonic educators are given as much authority, power, titles, and money as the ritualists, our Order is going to continue to suffer. Some day our leadership may awaken to this fact of life.

Viewpoint

The lead letter in FEEDBACK was written by a Brother "75½ years old and still going strong." I'd say he is "75½ years young." Of necessity his letter was condensed, but still contains the points he wanted to make. His points are certainly worth thinking about.

He's correct when he says "we have talked about education and then let it die on the vine." He wants to know why. In our "Note" we treated his "why?" too briefly. Why? Because we don't really have the answer. But part of the answer lies in our statement: "There's no limit to what Masonic education comprises."

For years I've been saying "THERE CAN BE NO DEDICATION WITHOUT EDUCATION." It's good to see this phrase being used more and more. But it's an empty phrase unless we do something to bring about dedication through education.

Grand Lodges have many, many excellent ritualists. Why? Because most Grand Lodges spend thousands of dollars every year to keep the ritual "pure." They usually depend upon men with other fulltime jobs to cover the other fields of Masonic education. Men are appointed to teach. They are given no instructions, no tools, no money to carry out the job they are appointed to do.

Common sense tells us teaching is a fulltime job. Yet, as far as I know, only one jurisdiction has a fulltime Director of Education. (Incidentally, this jurisdiction has a net gain in membership each year.) Industry doesn't depend upon volunteers to get jobs done. The company that did wouldn't last long. Millions of dollars are spent each year to train management and workers. Not to do so would be foolhardy.

In one jurisdiction a good Director of Education (who had to make a living in industry) submitted a budget for the following year. He asked for less than one-fifth the amount the ritual committee would spend. The Finance Committee didn't consult him. It simply reduced his request to less than one-fourth of what he had requested. He quit.

We're going to continue to discuss Masonic education. We're going to continue to point out ways to improve our leadership. We'll try to find the answer to Bill's "why?".

Another Reader Asks:

Q. Is it proper to give a copy of a Masonic book to a person who you would consider a good prospect for Masonry? Would this be considered indirect solicitation?

A. Yes, to part one; No, to part two. This should open the door to some honest differences of opinion. So let's go into our reasoning briefly. For over 200 years books about Freemasonry have been available to anyone interested in reading them. Many libraries are full of books critical of the Order. Many bookstores have anti-Masonic books prominently displayed. Most won't carry legitimate Masonic books because the demand for them doesn't exist. So the public gets a view of Freemasonry that is unflattering, to say the least. I have several of these books in my personal library, because we can't answer our critics unless we know what they are saying. Librarians won't buy good Masonic books because they aren't reviewed by the **New York Times, Publisher's Weekly,** or other sources they depend upon for their selections. On the other hand, librarians will accept gifts of books. Some Lodges make a regular practice of presenting good Masonic books to their local libraries. Many of them have received fine newspaper coverage, enhancing their position in the community. Isn't it better for us to pass out books that tell the truth about the Craft?

Solicitation is a touchy word. It is opposed and proposed with fury. What solicitation consists of varies with the individual. It's much like "morality." Who can define it accurately? I can't and won't attempt to. I would say, however, that giving a friend a Masonic book I enjoyed isn't an open invitation to him to ask for a petition. I'm proud of Freemasonry as a system that usually (but certainly not always) makes good men better. I want my friends to know why I'm proud of it. Perhaps this is the reason I've written books and produced films to tell the story accurately and truthfully. These books have been read and seen by thousands who aren't Freemasons. I am told many men became Master Masons because of them. I'm glad! Now, as for "solicitation," I'm opposed to it. I will be as long as we have a ballot box behind which men with petty grievances can hide.

A couple of years ago, while visiting some Freemasons in Maine and Rhode Island, I was asked what I thought about splitting the ritual and education between two officers. At that time the Grand Lecturer was charged with keeping the ritual pure, and teaching the Brethren the lessons behind the ritual.

There has never been any question as to how I feel. We can't serve two masters. Each of these are entirely different fields, although they are linked together. I suggested they be split. The following year they were. Now both Rhode Island and Maine have a Director of Education AND a Grand Lecturer.

Rhode Island in recent years was particularly fortunate. Grand Lecturer Charles Angel, and his successor (a close friend) Herbert McGuire, were good ritualists who firmly believed in Masonic education. Even so, both learned supervising both was too much for one man, or one committee (and I prefer to call these "teams").

Masonic Education in Rhode Island

HERBERT H. McGUIRE is the Grand Lecturer in Rhode Island. In this capacity he not only supervises the ritual but also Masonic education. It is with pleasure we note some of the concerns he has about the latter. "It is our belief," he wrote, "that the most important product we in Masonry have is our candidates. The life-blood of any Lodge, and thus Grand Lodge, lies in its candidates. If we foolishly turn our Lodges into 'degree mills', we shall rue the day. But we do need a steady influx of quality men to whom we can teach the ideals of Masonry and thus perpetuate our teachings and the Fraternity.

"We cannot teach our candidates unless we have knowledgeable Lodge Officers," he continued. In workshops "we try to teach him principles of Leadership, Management, Programming, Communication and many other facets of Masonic Education. . . .Everyone is afforded the opportunity to exchange ideas and problems and many potential problems are nipped in the bud. Attendance and participation by the Lodge Officers has steadily increased and we look at this as a healthy sign.

"We also believe that during the time a new Brother is taking his Symbolic Lodge Degrees we have an obligation to convince this candidate that he needs and wants what we in Masonry have to offer. If we can achieve this we shall have a Master Mason who will **want** to take an **active part.** An **Active** Mason means a **Vibrant Lodge** and our Craft will thus move forward."

Monthly "forums" are conducted. "In these Forums we teach the History of Masonry and the history and symbolism of each of the three degrees, as well as attempting to answer any questions the candidates may have. This is where the instructors sometimes learn many lessons themselves."

McGuire believes "that today's candidates are asking more questions and seeking more answers than in the past, and so we as Officers, are obligated to provide what they are searching for."

"If we are unable to excite them during this time," he continued, "they will take their three degrees and soon become disenchanted and never return. If we who are the educators of our Craft cannot arouse our new members, we will in time see our Craft disappear."

The basis for Rhode Island's educational program is the Masonic Leadership series of films of which there are five. These cover the fields of leadership, communication, planning, organizing and putting the right men in the right slots.

McGuire closed his comments by saying: "This is the 'Forward Look' as we see it in Rhode Island. We **do not** need to alter Masonry to conform to the standards of this or any other day. We **do need,** through Masonic Education, to teach our candidates the many valuable lessons and precepts contained in our ritual."

Several years ago the Grand Lodge of Tennessee took a far-reaching step. It became the first (and as far as I can determine, only) Grand Lodge to hire a full time Director of Masonic Education. John B. Arp, Jr., has done a fine job in this capacity. Something's being done right. This is one of the few Grand Lodges to have continuing net gains in membership.

This is what he has to say:

Freemasonry and Leadership:
Past, Present and Future

(Abstract of an article by John B. Arp, Jr., Director of Education for the Grand Lodge of Tennessee appearing in **Florida Mason)**

In the past we have been blessed with great leaders, men who were devoted to the principles in which we believe, and men who put these great principles into action in their daily lives. We are all familiar with the names and accomplishments of these individuals.

Although we recognize the creativeness of these brethren of the past, we must also recognize that the problems of the past still plague us. [Many of these problems were graphically pointed out through quotes from several Masonic leaders.]

Pick up any recent Grand Lodge Proceedings and I believe you will find that the leaders of today are still saying the same things that the leaders of thirty years ago said.

I am personally acquainted with Masonic leaders from several Grand Jurisdictions, and I know that Masonry is in good hands. I know that these brethren are capable, dedicated and devoted to their duty.

The time has come when our present day leaders must ask themselves the all-important question: Are we really serious when we say we need Masonic education and we want qualified leadership in our Lodges? **The key to will power is want power.** If we want something badly enough we will find the means to obtain it. Our present day leaders are in a position to make changes. The poet wrote: "Time turns the pages—the past is gone—and nature restores—the vanished years."

You and I, as leaders in our Fraternity, are in a position to stop talking about our needs and start doing something about them. We must make recommendations to our various bodies concerning Masonic education and Masonic leadership. We must have faith in our recommendations and the perseverance to stand by our convictions and see them become a reality. Joseph Fort Newton gave us this formula concerning faith. He said, "To live well we must have a faith to live by, a self fit to live with, and a work fit to live for." If we can, through our influence and efforts of today, produce outstanding Masonic leaders for tomorrow, is this not truly a work fit to live for?

These things we must do, if we expect to have future qualified leaders:

- Require that our officers have complete and comprehensive officers' training courses before they are eligible to hold an effective office in the Lodge.
- Insist on a Masonic educational program that reaches all segments of our Fraternity.
- Enforce the Masonic Law and stop turning our heads to violations of it; make the necessary changes to make the law more realistic and applicable.
- Exemplify the ritual in an impressive and creditable manner.
- The world will judge the tree by its fruit, so we must put into practice in our daily lives those precepts which are taught in the Lodge for this is the best way to attract new members and keep our Fraternity growing.
- To implement programs such as I have mentioned costs money. It will be the best investment a Masonic body can make. It will also take time to train leaders to train other leaders. It will be worth while and time well spent. Our business is making Masons and brothers through effective Masonic education, and with excellent Masonic leadership we can accomplish that goal.

Every year in almost every Grand Lodge the question of who's "the boss in Free-masonry" arises. While writing the history of the Grand Lodge of Ohio (Frontier Cornerstone) this question came up over and over again. Even though members of appendant bodies were openly reprimanded in Grand Lodge, or suspended from all rights and benefits of Freemasonry, the leaders of those bodies failed to get the message.

This problem can be covered at length, but what follows will give you a sampling of what's going on year after year throughout the country.

The Master Mason and The Grand Lodge

"I belong to a body that's higher than the Grand Lodge. I don't have to listen to anything it says." That's a comment heard in varying forms on too many occasions in too many places. Let's set the record straight.

For a Master Mason there is no Masonic-related body higher than the Grand Lodge. When it is not in session, there is no Mason "higher" than the Grand Master. He then becomes **the** Grand Lodge. To become a member of a body that erects itself from Master Masons, that is exactly what the member must be—a Master Mason. In every jurisdiction Master Masons come under the authority of that Grand Lodge.

The "number one" Mason in every jurisdiction is the Grand Master. There may be others in his presence who rule over more members of their bodies. Even so, he is first of all a Master Mason and comes under the authority of the Grand Master within whose jurisdiction he is residing or visiting. He, like all Master Masons, must obey the rules, regulations, and laws of that jurisdiction.

Several years ago the Virginia Craftsmen, a degree team that has gone almost all over the world, was visiting in Iowa. On the evening it was to exemplify the Master Mason Degree according to the Virginia ritual it learned a Fellowcraft was to be Raised. The President told the Worshipful Master the team couldn't do that. It didn't know the Iowa ritual. After rereading the Iowa Dispensation the President was still skeptical. So the Master brought the Grand Master to him. "I would like your fellows to Raise this Fellowcraft," said the Grand Master.

The President was in a dilemma! If the Iowa Fellowcraft was Raised by the Virginia Craftsmen it would violate the wording of the Virginia Dispensation. If the team couldn't Raise him, it would be violating the order of the Grand Master of Masons in Iowa. The President called his Grand Secretary (he knew his Grand Master wasn't available). The Grand Secretary, a Past Grand Master, was wise. He said, "You are in Iowa and the Grand Master has spoken. Raise the Fellowcraft!" He was!

To keep the name of the Grand Lodge and the appendant body, out of this actual case, I've changed the wording slightly. Not too long ago a Grand Master reported to his Grand Lodge:

"Lotteries seem to be peculiarly attractive to 'X'. During the year, at least two Xs involved themselves in these entanglements. In the case of one X, the matter was closed, in effect, before it came to the attention of the Grand Master. The other X was still engaged in carrying on its sale of tickets. I ordered that gambling activities be stopped at once. It was."

The last two words aren't exactly correct. The Grand Master was ignored. The sale of tickets went on. He called the head of X and asked why his order hadn't been obeyed. The head of X informed him who he was and that no Grand Master had jurisdiction over him. To which the Grand Master replied: "Do you want to continue to be the head of X?" "Certainly," he said. "Then," said the Master Mason, "stop the sales of those tickets immediately and refund every cent collected. If you don't you won't be a Master Mason tomorrow. If you aren't a Master Mason you can't be the head of X. And if there are others who persist in this illegal act, there will be an edict issued prohibiting any Master Mason from belonging to X organization." That made the last two words in his report correct.

Everyone is familiar with what happened to a Masonic-related organization in Pennsylvania. And everyone knows why it happened.

Recently a Grand Master, during his annual communication, strongly reprimanded the officers and members of a Lodge. It had been using a "short form" for the conferring of the Third, or Master Mason Degree. The excuse for not performing the degree as required by the Grand Lodge: "Other Lodges are doing it." The Grand Master said his requests for proof were not answered. At any rate, every Lodge in that jurisdiction knows now, if it didn't before, the laws of the Grand Lodge must be complied with.

Many similar, and worse, cases can be cited. But we are all familiar with them. Anyway, what's wrong with deciding for ourselves which laws we'll obey and which laws we'll disregard? Especially if those laws cause us to "waste time" or "keep us from raising funds for worthy causes." One word covers it all—everything.

If we don't like a Grand Lodge law we should take the legal steps necessary to change it. This can be done in every jurisdiction (with the possible exception of one). The way to do it is spelled out in the code of the Grand

Lodge. If the necessary majority of the voting members of the Grand Lodge agree with you, the law will be legally changed.

There must be harmony in every organization if it is to exist and grow. This is especially true in Freemasonry. We say so constantly. When we don't obey our laws, when we turn our backs on violations and violators, we destroy this harmony we must have.

So no one will get the wrong impression let me state for the record that I am a member of several appendant bodies. I'm proud to serve each of them. And I have in varying degrees. But I am first of all a Master Mason. This I must remain if I'm to continue to serve the other bodies. So must we all.

Public relations are important. Too often we forget that **internal relations** are even more important. Both can be, and have been, destroyed because some Master Mason didn't follow the laws of his Grand Lodge.

Let us remember that in Freemasonry there is no degree "higher" than that of Master Mason; there is no Masonic official "higher" than our Grand Master.

The Question that Brought About the Above

Q. I am concerned. I have heard pro and con arguments to the question that follows. I would like it settled once and for all. Here it is: I belong to an organization that requires a man to be a member of a lodge before he can belong to it. It holds raffles for either of three reasons: to aid its charitable project; for its building fund; or to help with current expenses. Is this legal? I should add, in my state it is against the law to gamble in any form. Please help.

A. You have really answered your own question. It's not giving away any of the few "secrets" of Freemasonry to say your organization is violating the obligations every Master Mason assumes. We have all promised to be law-abiding citizens; to protect the laws of our nation, state, and community; to obey the laws, rules, regulations, and edicts of our Grand Lodge. I know of no exceptions to this. To be certain, I've checked with at least 30 jurisdictions. In checking I've learned some startling things. There are Masonic-related bodies, and even some Lodges, that form auxiliaries, incorporate or do other things in an attempt to by-pass the laws of the Grand Lodge. I've also learned there are Grand Lodges (more accurately, officers) who "look the other way" so they won't have to get "involved." To stop such unlawful acts will make someone "unpopular." As Freemasons we **must** obey **all** laws. If we don't like the laws (and some are certainly foolish), we should take the **lawful** steps necessary to change them.

The late Walter Callaway, my good friend, edited the Masonic Messenger *of Georgia for several years. Since his death in 1977 that publication has become strictly an "in-house" periodical. Rarely does it contain a gem such as follows. Of this item Walt said: "Of all the farewell addresses, formal or informal, this writer has ever heard, one of the most eloquent summations was in December 1971."*

Frankly, I believe this tells more about the Masonic philosophy of Walter Callaway than anything I might write. It's the address of Charlton E. Clark of Solomon's Lodge No. 1, Savannah.

Laugh a Little, Cry a Little

Looking back, I ask myself, what does it mean to spend eight years in these chairs? It means a lot of things.

It means coming in as the Chaplain with high hopes of what you can do. Learning your opening and closing prayers and your degree prayers and committing the ritual to memory by etching every detail of it in your brain so that you can do it with hand on hip and foot in mouth.

It means serving out your years as steward and interminable sessions of coaching, in all sorts of places and under all sorts of conditions. I can remember in my years coaching in such assorted places as a lawyer's office, a barber shop, and at dear old Hunter Air Force Base. Back in the days of the Strategic Air Command when they would bring the base to full alert, some of those candidates would have to crawl under the fence to get to their coaching sessions, but they generally managed to make it somehow. It means coming across, as almost every coach does sooner or later, that one candidate who seems to disprove every established principal of the teaching and learning process.

It means standing in the cemetery in all weathers to pay your last respects to some dead and gone Brother whom you never knew, and some that you did know, good friends who have gone on; and trying to scrooch up under the undertaker's awning to keep the cold rain from running down the back of your neck.

It means turning out for funerals and rehearsals when there are clients waiting in the office whose business should have been transacted last week.

Like all important experiences in life, it means a combination of pleasure and pain. You laugh a little, and you cry a little. You live a little, and you die a little.

And finally and ultimately it means coming to the realization that your time is running out, as mine now is, like grains of sand slipping through your fingers, and you wonder where it all went. It is at such a time that one realizes that this Lodge of ours is greater than the sum total of all the men who ever belonged to it or who ever will, illustrious and noteworthy though some of them have been and undoubtedly will be in the future.

It is written in the Book of Ecclesiastes that one generation passes away and another takes its place, but the earth abides forever. I am firmly persuaded that for so long as the earth does abide in anything like its present form, our fraternity will endure regardless of what calamities may befall, even a wholesale nuclear holocaust, somewhere, in some crack or corner, Freemasonry will survive.

And thus it is that we come to at the end of this Masonic year, and the beginning of another, as we have for so many, many years.

If I could leave you with a parting thought, it would be this. I would paraphrase the immortal Mr. Pickwick when he said, "If I have done but little good, I hope I have done even less harm."

The question of race continually crops up in Freemasonry. It is a touchy subject. Actually there's no reason it should be. There's no color bar in Masonry. But there are fanatics (a mild term) on both sides of the line.
The article that follows covers, briefly, what's going on.

A Concerned Master
and Race

I recently started receiving "The Altar Light Newsletter." I am Worshipful Master of my Lodge, and I hold several appointed positions in my Grand Lodge. Since I've been affiliated with Freemasonry, I have been constantly amazed at the lack of association between the various factions within Masonry. I've read several publications concerning the origins or racial separation of Masons, but to date, I've read nothing to explain (officially) why they still remain separate.

Of course, as in "Society," Freemasons of different races tend towards separation. Why this remains so within Masonry, I don't know. In my obligation, there is nothing pertaining to the color of a man's skin, or to whether his is a 2-letter, 3-letter, 4-letter, or 5-letter man. I can, however, understand why those in power do not want to share that power, but why there isn't some concentrated effort to eliminate this problem, I'll never understand. It seems to me that there should be a conserted effort to recognize each other's faction as a legal entity within Freemasonry. We, as Freemasons, cannot continue repeating the mistakes of a bigoted general public. We must come together on one accord, that of a unified recognized union of Freemasons. There seems to be an organized effort to destroy Masonry, and now is the time to heal all divisions within our ranks.

If there is a question concerning being clandestine, someone should resolve this problem and bring about a much needed cohesiveness among Freemasons. Perhaps your readers may have some comments concerning this subject.

This letter raises some important questions. If this was an isolated case, we'd leave it alone. It isn't though. It's a question many Masonic leaders have been asked more times than they'd care to enumerate.

The writer wants to know why the races "still remain separate." In some respects it's a difficult question to answer, and may really have no answer, except the one he hints at. He does "understand why those in power do not want to share that power." I'm assuming (which is always dangerous) he's referring to those in official capacities on both sides of the "fence."

One item should be set straight. He notes that in his obligation "there is nothing pertaining to a man's skin." Exactly. Nothing in my obligation in Freemasonry prohibits me from accepting another man because of his color. Freemasonry is universally "color-blind." This is as it should be. I know of nothing that prevents a man of any color from petitioning and being accepted into any Masonic lodge in this country, or the world.

In March, I was the keynote speaker for a leadership seminar in New York. There were several black Masons present. They participated in the discussions and added pertinent information. In 1964, I was a guest of the Grand Lodge of Scotland for a Quarterly Communication. Many men of different colors were present as officials of Scottish Freemasonry. In 1976, I was a part of official Masonic receptions that included many Americans whose parents were Orientals. In between those years there have been many other Masonic episodes. So I can personally attest that there are men of differing colors, races, creeds, and religions in Freemasonry.

The writer notes further that "Freemasons of different races tend towards separation. Why this remains so within Masonry, I don't know." Again, I'm assuming he's referring to predominately "White Freemasonry" and "Black Freemasonry." During the early years of Freemasonry, Grand Lodges were troubled by splinter groups. This occurred in England as well as in this country. For over a century this hasn't been a problem among "White" or "Regular" Grand Lodges. The doctrine of exclusive Masonic jurisdiction has been established. This means there can be only one Grand Lodge in any State, or Masonic jurisdiction. It also means this doctrine will have to be changed if another Grand Lodge comprised of men of color, creed, or religion is to be allowed official recognition.

"Black Freemasonry" is still plagued by schisms. There are still many men belonging to "Grand Lodges." The only one of these Grand Lodges that can claim longevity is that bearing the name "Prince Hall." It's named in honor of a Black man who was made a Freemason in 1775 in Boston, Massachusetts. In 1784, Hall's Lodge, African No. 459 (later changed to 390), was granted a warrant by the Grand Lodge of England. Prince Hall died in 1807. In 1847 the name "Prince Hall Grand Lodge" was first used in New York. Much happened in between, and much has happened since. But since 1775 there has been Black Freemasonry associated with Prince Hall.

It is not my intention at this point to enter into a discussion of whether or not Prince Hall Masonry is legitimate. Brighter scholars than I'll ever be, on both sides, have been arguing this point for at least a century and a half. My objective is to listen to you. I've found our readers to be intelligent and well informed. And for the most part, they are unbiased.

Many writers leave behind unpublished works. Some are never intended to be printed. Some are written in haste and set aside to be refined. The status of what follows is difficult to determine, but having known Dr. James Noah Hillman intimately I believe he would approve of its publication here. He was deeply concerned about the need for good leadership.

During the last years of his life I had the honor to chauffeur Brother Hillman to many Masonic functions. On long lonesome drives all of us tend to "let our hair down." He was no exception. Many of the things discussed were never intended to be distributed, and they won't be. My Masonic education, in many fields, was enhanced by listening to his experiences. I will always cherish this association.

No Honors—No Innovations
—In Masonry

By James Noah Hillman

(Background: Among many papers discovered by the Curator of the George Washington Masonic National Memorial, William A. Brown, a Past Grand High Priest, was this "unfinished" manuscript written in the hand of Dr. James Noah Hillman. Why it wasn't finished and published, will never be known. It is an insight into the workings, or thinking of a man on the higher levels of authority in Freemasonry. From someone other than Hillman, we probably wouldn't consider publishing it. From a Mason of his qualifications, it carries considerable weight. Here's why.

He served as Grand Master of Masons in Virginia in 1938. In 1945 he was elected Grand Secretary of the Grand Lodge—the first Past Grand Master in Virginia's history to be elected to this position. He remained in it until late in 1958, when he resigned shortly before his death. The date actually was November 6, 1958, his 75th birthday.

Hillman was an educator in the public schools, at the College of Emory and Henry, and in Freemasonry. As Grand Master and as Grand High Priest he endeavored to raise the level of the thinking of Freemasons. He continued this work after he became Grand Secretary. He was the first Worshipful Master of Virginia Research Lodge, holding this position from 1950 to 1958.

He wrote countless papers and several Lodge histories. Prior to becoming Grand Secretary, he left Emory and Henry to assume the position of Director of Religious Education for the Methodist Church's Conference operating in Virginia and Tennessee.

On January 11, 1959, James Noah Hillman was buried with Masonic rites by his Grand Lodge in the Holsten Methodist Conference Cemetery at Emory.

The paper which follows, we are certain, Hillman would have refined and expanded. It is here presented as he left it.)

I am appalled. Yes, shocked, to put it mildly, at the near-sightedness of my Masonic Brothers who are associated with the Grand Lodges for asking the question, "What is the matter with Masonry?"

They continue to look for someone else on whom to place the blame, when they themselves are creating the downfall of Masonry in the Subordinate Lodges. They have long forgotten the fact that the Subordinate Lodge can not exist without a Grand Lodge, but a Grand Lodge cannot exist without the Subordinate Lodges.

Thomas Jefferson, while President of the United States, wrote: "Beware of energetic governments, they are always oppressive."

Thus it has become noticeable in the Grand Lodges. They, too, are becoming oppressive. Each year they build their regulations, rules and laws upon the Subordinate Lodges.

Many of the Masters are ignorant of the fact that they are the Master of their Lodge by the vote of the membership and even a Grand Master has no real authority over them when it comes to the governing of their Lodge, as long as they abide by the rules and regulations of Masonry set down by the vote of their peers.

In the beginning, and at the foundation of Masonry, it is written in the rules of the Constitution that there shall be no honors in Masonry, for we are all to meet on the level. Also it is written that there shall be no innovations in Masonry. Yet for the past 40 years of my life, and probably for the hundreds of years before that, the Grand Lodges have continually made innovations and have built false importance around the officers and members of the Grand Lodge.

When we open our Lodges and take inventory, we find very few Master Masons, but the attendance is packed with titled Master Masons, and those who have come for personal honors.

Yet! they say, "What is the matter with Masonry?" They do not look at themselves and what they are a party to. I doubt if they would take the time to question members of the younger generation on the reason they no longer look to the Masonic Fraternity as something to emulate.

As for constructive criticism, may I suggest the following for your consideration?

First, let us destroy the present book of Rules and Regulations with its oppressive laws, and pick up the book of Rules and Regulations as it was written just 150 years ago.

Second, let us no longer introduce or give honors, except the visitor be unknown to the members, and should be introduced. Nothing is so boring to the Master Mason than to witness the endless stream of introductions and the marching to the East to receive so-called honors. How some appear to puff themselves up with importance and no longer remember their obligations to the true principals of Masonry—"Friendship, Morality and Brotherly Love."

Third, if you cannot remember them all, at least let us remember and never forget "Brotherly Love." Forget yourself and try to look for ways to help your Brother Master Mason.

After all, importance is a matter of semantics.

When you try to make yourself important, you are only important to yourself, but when you help your Brother, you become important to others. The first is buried with you—the second you leave behind.

Note: This paper was read in Virginia Research Lodge No. 1777, AF&AM, on December 9, 1978. The favorable response was overwhelming. A Past Grand Master said it should be widely published. *The Altar Light* agrees. At the same time we would add a caution. Brother Hillman would never be a party to a rebellion. He knew well that today all Lodges must hold a Charter from the Grand Lodge in its jurisdiction to operate legally. He also knew there must be laws, rules and regulations and customs or there will be complete chaos. Within this framework, the "evils" he mentions can be corrected.

This remarkable letter was written by a Canadian Entered Apprentice. *It is amazing when we consider few Master Masons have grasped the teachings of the Craft as had this man who had received only one degree. In his covering letter to me he said: "I believe that every Mason should stand up and be counted whenever any slanderous statements are made about Masonry."*

I have long felt the same way. However, I realize there are more than two schools of thought on this subject. There are those who believe attacks on the Craft should go unanswered. They feel the more one "stirs mud the dirtier it gets." That's true—insofar as mud is concerned. But even though an ostrich buries its head (so it's claimed) at the first sign of danger, the danger doesn't go away.

During the period of the Morgan craze in the 1830's Freemasonry was persecuted and almost became extinct. It wasn't until years after its beginning that some of the Masonic leadership started striking back. When it did, the cowards in the anti-Masonic groups turned their heels and ran, as all cowards do.

Many so-called religious factions have been and are radically opposed to Freemasonry. They spread slander constantly. We're inclined to overlook what they are saying and doing, hoping they will stop. They won't. In the meantime they are causing one of the few truly tolerant organizations untold harm.

Not too long ago a member of a local Lodge informed me he'd have to renounce Masonry. The new church he was attending found Masonry unsuitable for Christians. A month before he should have been elected Worshipful Master, a Senior Warden wrote a letter of resignation. He had become a "born again Christian" and his church found nothing in Freemasonry a Christian could support.

Perhaps it's time for our Masonic leadership to rethink its position.

A Letter from An Entered Apprentice

Dear Worshipful Sir:
I trust that this letter reaches you in good health. May I take this

opportunity to discuss with you a topic of mutual interest and indeed of mutual concern. As an Entered Apprentice Mason, always seeking more Light, I naturally turn to my cherished Masonic Holy Bible of which your signature as Master is therein. Esoterically speaking, it is here that I will find further knowledge of our Craft and its Mysteries.

To augment my Biblical readings, I have sought out further esoteric articles and it is here that I unfortunately have to report to you, Worshipful Sir, a rather unpleasant experience. I noticed on the newsstands a special centennial edition of a magazine. . . .which I enclose a copy of an article. . . .which I find personally offensive.

The point I wish to make about this farcical article is one of the image it conjures to the highly gullible general public, and what long range effects it may have? After reading the article this writer is convinced that journalist. . . .is completely void of any true understanding of Masonic Obligations nor our cherished tenets, being Brotherly Love, Relief and Truth.

[This] deceptive, contemptible article lacks any sensitivity or diplomacy, but also includes the journalistic cardinal sin of failure to understand and cope with proper investigative journalism. For an example, he uses the trite expression for the Craft as "an engine for conspiracies" when the truth is that one of the prime Masonic teachings is to Support the existing Government bravely, honourably and politely always respecting the "Ties of Blood and Relationship."

For those non-intellectuals who like boredom with a touch of paranoia, I highly recommend written articles such as [this]. At times I found it difficult to remain calm for in the past my sympathies have always laid with young, inexperienced journalists and their struggle to keep their heads above water. This includes publishers as well! But, I was apalled by such sensationalism at the expense of a time honoured fraternity such as ours!

It is my personal opinion that a society or fraternity that turns its back on its own history can truly be said to be in an advanced stage of decline, and the failure of its members or brethren on this occasion to act on its own account can be properly considered a cause of fraternal conviction. This centennial edition's main cover story could have been pleasantly and graciously treated but it was done with express scorn and not in a genuine manner.

I could hear my pulse beat when [he] mockingly ridiculed various aspects of our obligations but to suggest, as the cover will indicate, "Who shot J.F.K." was really going for the jugular. Page after page, [he] pounds out his message with all the subtlety of a jack-hammer—that of having contempt for the Craft. I personally believe that Character determines Destiny, thus I truly fear for [his] future.

Instead of raising Hell, or being nasty, [he] should constantly check for accuracy, write genuine, as opposed to counterfeit, pseudo articles, always endeavoring to practice Charity and Benevolence. Perhaps someone with tact should explain that:

a Mason is obliged to obey the moral Law; he will never be a stupid Atheist; or an irreligious Libertine; to be good Men and True. . . . whatever Denomination or Persuasion they may be—distinguished men of Faith.

I need not point out to you, Worshipful Sir, the article's many inaccuracies, witless wrongs, pointless slang, erroneousnesses and injustices. On the other hand, the article—in places—is well written, interesting and has a considerable amount of merit, but due to its tone and trite style, the author has reduced it to a mundane level and hence I would not recommend it as informative or enjoyable reading.

Pretum Laborum Non Vile

Richard H. Curtis has been the editor of The Northern Light, *the official publication of the Northern Jurisdiction of the Scottish Rite, for a number of years. In this capacity he has been able to pass along good and wholesome advice to his readers. This advice I consider to be excellent.*

What Do Masons Know About Masonry

By Richard H. Curtis, Editor, "The Northern Light"

Soon the cry will be "School's out!" and the local press will carry a photo of jubilant students bouncing out of the classroom in pure delight. Such a photo is a classic for the month of June.

Other familiar scenes reflect graduates at commencement exercises throwing their caps in the air and shouting "I made it!"

At the conclusion of the degree of Master Mason, there appears to be a similar expression of jubilation. Frequently the new member is congratulated by the Worshipful Master and told he is now as much a Mason as he ever will be. The new Master Mason says to himself, "I made it!" His brief journey from Entered Apprentice to Master Mason was merely a matter of months and probably was not strenuous. Too often we find that not much was expected of him as a candidate and much less will be asked of him as a "full-fledged" member. What a shame! If he did not learn the basics as he advanced, how can he possibly pass on his Masonic knowledge to another generation?

Being "made" a Mason does not necessarily "make" an *intelligent* Mason of anyone. One of the biggest tasks facing the fraternity today is the fact that Masonic "students" must be encouraged to learn.

Too many Lodges rely on the mere recitation of lectures with phraseology which is not necessarily the style of our day-to-day conversation. If the Masonic ritual is "untouchable," then we must supplement the ritual by using other means of communicating the precepts of Freemasonry. But the end result must bring about a more knowledgeable Mason.

If a new Mason is not inspired to seek more light in Masonry, he will become nothing more than a part of the annual statistics. The next time you witness the third degree, take a good look at the new Master Mason and ask yourself this question: "Is he ready to build a 'cathedral'?"

If your answer to the question is "no," then take him aside and help him to use the working tools. Better yet, let it not happen to the next candidate. Get back to that lodge for the first degree. Encourage the new Entered Apprentice to gain a deeper understanding of the Masonic philosophy. Offer to assist with instruction. Teaching, you know, is a great way to broaden one's own knowledge.

If your answer to the above question is "yes," you may have found a lodge that is doing something right. Or perhaps you've been mesmerized into accepting lower standards. If the latter is the case, then you'd better rush back to your lodge and start yourself over again as an Entered Apprentice—before your "cathedral" crumbles.

Masonic Feast

A Lost Tradition? was written by PGM Dean Tillotson, and was carried in *Arizona Masonry*. It's too good to condense. Here it is in full:

As Freemasonry has changed throughout the years, one of the things we have lost seems to be the "Festive Board" which was part of Masonry in the eighteenth century. Dr. George Oliver, distinguished Mason, cleric and author wrote in 1854 in his book "Revelations of a Square" the following:

"There was a festive gratification thrown over a Masonic banquet which was unapproachable by any other society. It was not in the viands (they are the same anywhere), it is not the wines—we cannot boast of any superiority there. The secret may be found in the congeniality of feeling which mutually exists among the brethren—knit together by closer ties—cemented by a chain of more sincere and disinterested affection—each and all being determined to give and receive pleasure—to be happy themselves, and the source of happiness to others. "By this means a Lodge of true-hearted brothers, during its hours of relaxation or refreshment, is a region of peace, and the patented abode of good temper and an occasional bowl of chili served at such a late hour that many of the Craft are already up past their normal bed-time does not fit the definition of a Feast. And the conversation is usually limited to a few remarks by the Master and the Candidate; this does not fit either. Nor does the occasional dinner that might be served before Lodge; at these the brothers are usually subjected to a long discourse by a visiting fireman which rarely, if ever, adds to their Masonic knowledge or to an interminable list of introductions of men whom they already know and have been introduced to over and over in the past. In each case, there is little opportunity for real discourse because too soon it becomes time to open Lodge.

I hope to see the day when some enterprising Master might call his meeting for 6:00 p.m., see to it that business or degree was conducted with alacrity, and then call the Lodge to refreshment for a FEAST. Perhaps he might even be astute enough to have a few brothers primed to give a few short remarks on what Masonry means to them and to end the meal with a toast or two to the Craft and a song. He might then begin to approach the feelings of har-

189

mony and friendship as was experienced two centuries ago.

H. L. Haywood, a popular Masonic author of this century, said in 1948, "It is written in the first paragraph of the account of the founding of the Mother Grand Lodge in 1717 . . . .that the old Lodges in London has two (and only two) purposes in constituting a Grand Lodge. One was to establish a center of union and harmony, the other was to revive the Quarterly Feasts.

"Why Feasts? Because then (as it had been for centuries) the Feast stood close to the heart of the Lodge, was one of the fundamental things in the Lodge."

Have we, in Arizona and the United States today, lost one of the fundamental joys of Masonry that our ancient brothers loved so much?

I've often been accused of living in the past more so than in the present. This isn't exactly true. I live in the present, although I do write about the past. I've found history does repeat itself, often in a different disguise. When we take away the mask we find much that's happening today also occurred in the past. We can't understand the present, or prepare for the future, unless we understand the past.

The one thing we can't do is live on our past laurels. We've got to get off our duffs and make the present as important as the past. We extoll the virtues of many leaders who were Freemasons hundreds of years ago—Washington and Franklin, for instance. We must develop the same type of leaders today and tomorrow if Freemasonry is to survive.

We're told this is difficult to do now. There are too many distractions. Too many things are vying for the time of men. It's difficult earning a living. Hogwash! There were many more distractions in the lives of our forefathers than there are today. Until recent years it took hours, even days, to travel short distances. Now it takes minutes. We can travel across the country in less than six hours. Modern equipment has made it possible to do in minutes what it took days, even months, to accomplish. We've got the time, but do we have the inclination? Do we have the dedication?

Frankly, I believe the only reason Freemasonry isn't a much more powerful organization for good is because our leaders have let us down. They don't understand the past and have no idea where we should be going in the future. They're content not to "rock the boat." It takes time and effort to lead and teach. It's much easier to sit back and go along with the tide.

How can men be dedicated to something they know nothing about? They can't. Until we learn and pass along the wealth that is Freemasonry, the dedication we need won't exist.

Is The Past Important?

Recently I received a hard-hitting letter from a charter subscriber to *The Altar Light*. He said he still enjoyed the newsletter, "but it seems to be getting away from what brought it the most success—that is, breaking new ground, and informing on subjects *no other publishers* would touch." The emphasis is his.

He mentioned some of the areas we've covered over the past four years. Actually, we're still covering them. But we don't want to sound like a broken record. And this could easily happen. Many of these problems could be mentioned over and over again. At any rate we'll continue to "break new ground" whenever we believe it's necessary.

Our friend also noted he's not as interested in the past as he is in the present. How often we've heard that. Yet the past is important. Without knowing where we've been we often don't know where we should be heading into the present. Then, too, much that happened in the past should be repeated in the present.

Let's consider the present for the moment. Our Lodges and Grand Lodges have abdicated much they should be doing over to appendant bodies. This wasn't always the case—and this is where knowing something about the past can come in mighty handy. What am I referring to? FUN! Before many of the appendant bodies came on the scene, our lodges provided fun for their members. I'm not talking about Tomfoolery. I'm talking about feasts, Table Lodges, family and community affairs.

Music once was a familiar scene at many Masonic functions. We've gotten away from the joy of singing and musical instruments. Why not get back to it? If not the lodges, why not the districts? It has been done in rare instances with great success.

Table Lodges are beginning to make their reappearance. But not as often as they should. It's an excellent opportunity for Masons to feast, have fellowship, sing, learn, and thoroughly enjoy Freemasonry.

We'll have more to say on this subject of "fun" later. It's not too late or too early, for you to start the fun rolling. Do it. You'll be surprised at the reception you'll receive from your Brother Masons.

This article appeared in The Pennsylvania Freemason. *It isn't signed, but it sounds just like our good friend William A. Carpenter, Deputy Grand Master. We're repro-ducing it here because far too many good men ask about Freemasonry—and are told nothing. Why? We fear it's because too many Master Masons know so little about the Craft they're afraid to say anything. If the advice in this article can't be followed, please bring the questioner into contact with a well-informed Brother. You'll be doing the questioner and Freemasonry a favor.*

What Should We Say If Asked About Freemasonry?

What should we tell our non-Masonic friends when they ask questions about Freemasonry?

When these questions arise, and they often do, our response will undoubt-edly influence the mental attitude of our friends toward ourselves and the Craft in general.

We should not take a timid approach to our answers. We should not indi-cate a desire to "change the subject." We should not reflect a "mum's-the-word" attitude.

Instead, we should be prepared to speak with ease, pride and authority.

Make it known that Freemasonry is a way of life.

Freemasonry is fraternal in organization, religious in character, based on the belief in the Fatherhood of God, Brotherhood of Man and the Immortality of the Soul.

Be prompt to make it known that Freemasonry is not a "secret society" as many surmise. Freemasonry is a voluntary association wherein the interested one comes of his own free will and accord.

Indicate also that Freemasonry is not a religion as many claim it is.

Discussions on religion or politics have no place in our proceedings.

Proclaim that Freemasonry, in its every effort and purpose strives to do charitable work within its membership and for society, and through its teach-ings, seeks to make good men better men. You can proudly state that the basic ethical principles as exemplified in our Ritual and Lodge Work, are such as are most acceptable to all good men; they are lessons based on the golden rule, tolerance toward men, respect for one's family, charity towards all and being true to God for His gracious and numerous blessings.

Be proud to proclaim that Freemasonry is a band of men bound together in the bonds of Brotherly Love and Affection that extends throughout the World.

And to sum it all up Freemasonry is kindness in the home, honesty in business, courtesy in society, fairness in work, pity and concern for the unfortunate, resistance toward the wicked, help for the weak, trust in the strong, forgiveness for the penitent, love for one another and, above all, reverance and love for God.

These and many other answers can be applied to the questions your friends will ask.

Speak up. What do we have to hide—save that which pertains to our esoteric Work?

Freemasonry is a Way of Life?

What follows is what one Grand Lodge is doing to change the image of Free-masonry in its country. What is proposed didn't take place overnight, nor did the proposals come easy. Even its publication, The New Zealand Freemason, *will change. It will be published quarterly and increased in size from 16 to 24 pages.*

The chairman of the Editorial Board noted: "The move to present the Craft as an institution to be interpreted to those inside and outside is not to satisfy a whim but to acknowledge a necessity. Not all will applaud such a move but as time goes on most will accept it." He added that only articles of national interest will be published. "Who in Northland wants to read of an event in a lodge meeting in Southland or vice versa?" I hope he won't be dogmatic on this point. Once in a while what happens in one area can be of the utmost importance anywhere. Our "Through Masonic Windows" proves this. Of course, we have only carried items of international interest there. Local elections and awards for longevity, such as 50 year pins and certificates, have no interest outside the locality.

The chairman closed his editorial by stating: "To remain successful the winds of change cannot be ignored and this new move is notice to all that for the present, change is the name of the game."

Not only the publication will change, so will the image of the whole Grand Lodge.

The Winds of Change
(A Brief Report from *The New Zealand Freemason*)

During the Annual Communication of the Grand Lodge publicity and internal education were thoroughly discussed. The External Relations Committee was disturbed. It had received little cooperation. It had been unsuccessful in obtaining coverage in the mass media.

Those present were asked how many knew "the Craft had given $5,000 to the Southland flood relief campaign and $10,000 to the Abbotsford disaster fund." The response indicated the committee had a difficult job ahead.

The committee reported it would be concerned with every phase of communication. This would include paid advertising and free publicity in "all the media outlets." It would provide a "framework for the achievement of these objects by the publicity committees which every Provincial Grand Master had been asked to set up."

And "unless the Craft was prepared to become outgoing and abandon many of its restrictive attitudes to letting the 'outside world' know what it stood for and what it did, then its future was a dismal one."

The discussion proved there was "widespread approval of what the committee was trying to achieve. It was noted that notices of meetings had been placed in hotels and motels in some areas, and the response had been great. Times and dates of meetings had been placed on a "notice board" in another area and this "was certainly helpful for tourists and other visitors who might wish to attend a meeting."

"A theme which was repeated more than once during the seminar was that Freemasonry was the most criticised body in New Zealand because it did not tell people what it did. And another, judging by the murmurs of assent had the approval of many delegates, was that although they would return home and tell their members about the two committees which had been set up, it was no good trying to 'sell' the new image to the public 'until we have sold it to ourselves'."

This the "Internal Education Committee" was going to attempt. But it was noted the ways and means of "Masonic education had to be flexible." It was noted "it would be impossible to impose a strict regime from above."

There were comments "about the reactionary attitude of many older members in the East. Too many old past members 'tried to put a damper on everything.' "

It was also noted: "Changes were taking place in the Craft regardless of what anyone thought and the education of the brethren to new ways and new attitudes was the major task to be faced."

"Freemasons must learn to acknowledge their membership to the outside world. We have got to be Freemasons. Let us forget about being shy and hesitant."

What is taking place in New Zealand has taken place in a few areas in the United States. The "winds of change" should take place in every jurisdiction. It is way past time for the public to learn about the good works of Freemasonry.

This follows what I discussed a little earlier. There isn't much I can add to what I wrote then, nor what's covered here.

A copy of this article, along with a covering letter was sent to the publisher of the Virginia newspaper that carried the item referred to. By return mail I received a brief statement from the publisher. He said the reporter was no longer with the paper. He didn't say when, why or how he left. Let's hope for the sake of honest journalism he found another field in which to make his living.

"Turn The Other Cheek"

Rarely has Freemasonry answered its many critics. Its policy appears to have been for centuries to "turn the other cheek." A recent Grand Master refused to let his Public Relations Chairman answer a vicious attack on the Craft. "The more you stir mud, the more it stinks," he claimed.

Is he correct? Should Freemasonry let false statements circulate? If so, where do these untruths stop?

Here's an example of a recent newspaper feature story.

"The man enters a room full of solemn faced men and as the heavy door shuts behind him, he is told to remove his clothing. Then he is blindfolded and a cable is placed around his neck.

"He is made to stand, sit and pose in various awkward positions to test his stamina and concentration, as the conveyors of the ritual begin to unfold a series of stories and allegories that set forth their own code of morality.

"If he 'acts up', he'll be jerked out by the cable, thrown naked into the streets and banished from his secret society."

These are the beginning paragraphs of the feature story read by thousands of non-Masons. If you knew little or nothing about Freemasonry, would you want to join such a "secret society"? I certainly wouldn't!

You and I know the "reporter" doesn't know what he's talking about. The public doesn't. We know no candidate strips naked; the "cable" is a cord and no man has ever been "jerked" by one and "thrown naked into the streets." No candidate is put in "awkward positions." On the contrary, every candidate is made to feel comfortable and put at ease.

A little later we find another outright lie. "George Washington was a Mason [true] as were most of the founding fathers [false] and half the U.S.

197

Presidents [false]. Washington headed the first lodge established in this country [in 1733!, a year after his birth?], and no doubt took the noble knife on many occasions to make sure the initiate was human, to see if he bleeds." How ridiculous can a writer get? Never has an initiate been made to bleed— never did Washington officiate in a Masonic Lodge, or Grand Lodge. True, he was the Charter Worshipful Master of Alexandria Lodge No. 22, Alexandria, Virginia. That was in 1788, and he was elected the following year. BUT, he never did preside over the Lodge.

This reporter tells us something every Masonic historian has searched for and been unable to discover until now!

"What can be said for certain is that Masonry flourished in Egypt during the days of pyramid construction and worship of gods such as Isis, Osiris and Ra. Then Masonry moved to Europe where the same rituals were applied to the Christian religion and the same techniques to the construction of great cathedrals."

Eureka! We have found the answer! There's only one problem. Where was Masonry between the time of the building of the pyramids and the beginning of Christianity?

No legitimate newspaper should keep a reporter on its payroll if he doesn't check his facts. Let's be charitable and believe this one did check out the above through exposés and a "member who provided the account of the initiation." Even though it's impossible to believe, let's give him the benefit of the doubt. That's more than he gave the Craft. Several items he reported could have been checked easily. For instance:

"The most famous controversy Masons were involved with came after the publication in 1826 of William Morgan's 'Illustrations of Masonry.' [False. It started before the publication.] Morgan, once a Mason [false, he never was], revealed many of the initiation secrets in his book [this statement is qualified so we can't say it's true or false].

"Soon after the book appeared, Morgan vanished [false, he disappeared before it was published] and many argued he was done in by the Masons, an argument given some credence by the fact that the publisher's printing building was burned the next night [false] and a year later Morgan's body was found in the sands of a Lake Ontario beach [false, Morgan was never located]." These are facts readily found in any legitimate account of the Anti-Masonic Party, a political organization of dubbed or unscrupulous politicians.

"Lafayette, the French general, was given a cold shoulder when he first arrived and began to assert himself. As one historian wrote, 'Lafayette was not accepted until he joined a Masonic lodge.' " This "reporter" doesn't name "one historian." Any of us can find "historians" with the point of view we want to promote. In any case, this statement is utterly false. Lafayette was a Freemason before he came to America. This is the best information we can find. We know for certain he wasn't made a Mason in this country, but in France.

Interestingly enough, the "reporter" has kind words to say about the Elks and the Moose; nothing but slander for Freemasonry.

About a year ago I was handed six photocopied pages of an article from some magazine entitled "Your Daddy Was a Weirdo." This is even more slanderous than the article noted above from the newspaper. In bold print in the middle of several pages it claims:

"After he was tortured according to the Master Mason's oath he had sworn, Captain Morgan came to rest on the bottom of the Niagara River wearing the early American equivalent of cement galoshes."

"The Masons are Laurel and Hardy heading for the Shriners' Convention to escape their wives and booze it up. . . .Fred Flintstone greeting Barney Rubble with the secret word of the Water Buffalo, 'ak-ak-a-dak.' "

"When Harry Truman said he knew no secrets, he really said that the only secret is secrecy, see?"

This article is so full of falsehoods it will take several pages to answer them.

Should Freemasonry continue "turning the other cheek"? Should Freemasonry continue to let slanderous statements remain unchallenged?

During the so-called "Morgan Affair" Freemasonry did just that for years. During those years it suffered. In fact, it almost died. It wasn't until a few Grand Lodges said "enough" and fought back by telling the truth. It didn't take long for the Craft to rebound once some of the leaders took off the gloves and stopped turning the other cheek.

And don't think for a single moment there can't or won't be another anti-Masonic craze. The articles noted herein prove there are still many anti-Masonic nuts floating around.

This account of the 200th anniversary of the Grand Lodge of Virginia is repro-
duced for one purpose only—to show what can happen when constructive leadership
takes the reigns. The Bicentennial Committee was in existence for nine years before
the obstructionists were forced by the press of events to let others do the job that
should have been done earlier.

Perhaps what's recorded here will help one Grand Lodge or Lodge to avoid some
of the pitfalls that are noted.

A Gala Celebration

It was an outstanding event—but it was almost a disaster. This was the
200th Anniversary of the Grand Lodge of Virginia, Ancient, Free and Accepted Masons.

It was on October 13, 1778, when a Masonic Convention finally decided it
was legal to elect a Grand Master for Virginia. For 18 months representatives
from five of the known 12 Lodges in Virginia wrestled with the problem. The
result was the election of John Blair, Jr., to be the first Grand Master of
Masons in Virginia.

Blair wasn't the first choice. It is claimed George Washington was. Perhaps so, but the only evidence is a purported statement saying he would be a
"proper person to fill the office." No record exists showing he was asked and
declined, as has been claimed. Even so, the Grand Master of Masons in
Virginia wears a jewel which an engraver claimed was made for Washington.

The first choice of the Convention for Grand Master was Warner Lewis of
Botetourt Lodge of Goucester Courthouse. He declined. His reason, it is
said, was because his sympathies were with England. So John Blair, Jr., of
Williamsburg Lodge was the unanimous choice of the Convention. After his
selection, the Convention adjourned until October 30, 1778, when it would
again meet to install Blair and the officers he chose to serve with him.

The Capital of Virginia was moved from Williamsburg to Richmond in
1780. That year the Grand Lodge held its last meeting in Raleigh Tavern in
Williamsburg and Chartered its first entirely new Lodge, Richmond No. 13,
later changed to No. 10.

Because of the war, and perhaps because there was no suitable place to meet, no Communications were held until 1784. The Grand Lodge has met every year since.

No celebration was held for its 100th Anniversary. The then Grand Master felt the money it would take could be better used to help the victims of "a pestilence that walketh in darkness."

Grand Master H. Bruce Green, on February 13, 1968, recommended plans be started for a Bicentennial Celebration, and an assessment of twenty-five cents per member be collected for the next ten years. The Grand Lodge agreed. But it wasn't until 1971 a Bicentennial Committee was appointed. L. Douglas Delano, who would become Grand Master in 1976, was appointed Chairman. He would hold this position through the Bicentennial year of 1978.

The *Altar Light,* believing it will be a service to Freemasonry in general, asked the Chairman to tell us some of the valuable lessons he learned. We also asked Walter J. "Jerry" Harmon, Chairman of the Public Relations Committee of the Grand Lodge of Virginia, to add his comments. For obvious reasons, nothing controversial will appear in this interview.

The Altar Light: What I'd like for us to do, Doug and Jerry, is pass along to Lodges and Grand Lodges some of the things learned from the long years of work for the Bicentennial of the Grand Lodge of Virginia. Doug, you had a large committee to work with. How was it selected? What was taken into account?

L. Douglas Delano: It was appointed by the then Grand Master. He tried to select men of varying degrees of knowledge, and men from every geographical area of the state.

AL: You lost men over the years through death, resignations, and for other reasons, I assume. How were these replaced?

LDD: The Grand Master would usually go along with my recommendations. I should say that we added the leaders of the larger appendant bodies. Then, too, as new Grand Lodge officers were elected, they were added to the committee.

AL: Was any criteria used to select these men other than their being officers?

LDD: Yes. The Chairman of our Committee on Art was one; another was from the oldest Lodge in Virginia.

AL: None were chosen because of their special expertise?

LDD: Not particularly, but I must point out those who took on special jobs did them well.

AL: Would it have helped to have had men with expertise?

LDD: We found out later this was true, because we had to call on them. Two are here now—Jerry and you.

AL: We'll come back to that. What was the first thing your committee did?

LDD: Go to Williamsburg! That was in 1971. If we hadn't we wouldn't have been able to meet there. The hotels have to be booked up years in advance. So does the convention center. If we had waited even another month, there would have been no meeting in Williamsburg.

AL: Did the committee set any goals?

LDD: One of the first things we wanted was our history, but for varying reasons, we didn't get it. Then, another thing we wanted to do was place historical markers about the state. We ran into governmental blocks there, so this wasn't done. I'd still like to see this done.

AL: Did you have sub-committees working on different items?

LDD: Yes, this was necessary. We had them working on housing, obtaining and packaging mementos, and although he wasn't a member of the Bicentennial Committee, Jerry was Chairman of Public Relations. Fortunately, he had a good background in the entertainment field. He saved us from disaster in this area.

AL: How?

LDD: We had a fine group signed up, we thought, to provide the entertainment for the Bicentennial Celebration during the Annual Communication in February. About a year before the Communication, it backed out. We didn't know what to do, so we turned to Jerry. So, a committee of this type must have someone on it who is knowledgeable about entertainment, and all it covers.

AL: How did you keep the Lodges and the Masons of Virginia informed about the Bicentennial?

LDD: Mainly through our statewide publication *The Masonic Herald.* And we sent correspondence periodically to the Lodges with information to be read to the members. I should mention at this point I saw your *"Saga of the Holy Royal Arch of Freemasonry"* and liked what I saw. I mentioned this to the committee. We viewed the film, then commissioned you to produce a Bicentennial motion picture for us. We were able to arouse considerable interest in the members by letting them know about this.

AL: What were some of the highlights of this celebration?

LDD: Your film, *"Challenge!"* has to top the list because it's something of lasting value; the mural added so much to the Communication in Williamsburg and the ten area celebrations this year; the presentation of the John Blair Medal to the College of William and Mary; the time capsule; the mementos; the presentation of the James Mercer portrait to the Virginia Supreme Court; the displays carried throughout the state.

AL: How was attendance at those ten area meetings?

The last meeting of the Grand Lodge of Virginia before moving to the new capital of Richmond was held in Raleigh Tavern, Williamsburg, 1780.

This is a scene from Challenge!

LDD: Not as good as we would have liked, but better than for most Masonic events.

Walter J. Harmon: Let me inject this. Considering all the things available to men today, the attendance was good.

AL: You, Jerry, or a member of your Public Relations Committee, filmed these events in Super 8, didn't you?

WJH: We did. This footage will be of untold value in years to come. We also filmed much of the proceedings of the 200th year in Williamsburg.

AL: Jerry, you started to say something when we were talking about attendance. What was it?

WJH: I think we use the wrong yardstick when we measure attendance. There are many more activities today than there were 50 years ago. These things are touching every organization.

LDD: That's right. Fifty years ago people would have flocked to these events. I must add here that every showing of *"Challenge!"* was filled to capacity. You know the reception it received in Williamsburg, and it was just as good all over the state.

AL: Were you pleased with the attendance at Williamsburg in February?

LDD: Indeed I was! And we had Grand Masters from something like 35 states, all over Canada, plus England and Southern Africa. I haven't heard of anyone who didn't rave about the whole celebration.

AL: What would you suggest those who are going to have a large-scale celebration do?

LDD: Start years in advance. There are some things that can't be done early, but if you get the things that can be settled, you'll be in good shape for the things that have to wait. For instance: your motion picture couldn't wait until the last minute; a history has to be started years in advance. [This history has never been written!]

AL: If you sign up your entertainment too early, Jerry, can you get in trouble?

WJH: The committee found that out. I would say two years before, if possible, certainly a year in advance. And don't use small booking agents. Go to the big ones. Don't forget, good entertainers are booked at least a year in advance and often two.

AL: Did you gain, Doug, by the change in entertainment?

LDD: Indeed we did. But we were fortunate to have Jerry with his vast background come to our rescue. He was able to give the committee a choice of topnotch entertainers. From them we selected Ethel Merman. And you know what happened. Almost every seat in the large William and Mary Hall was filled, and she brought down the audience. They loved her. She saw this and gave them an extra half hour.

AL: Was the building suitable for the entertainment selected?

WJH: No! And that's something the planners should take into consideration. Another building might have cost more, but if you have to bring in sound equipment, lights, backdrops, and the multitude of items necessary for a successful show, the building costing more to rent may be the least expensive in the long run. We had to bring in all those things and more.

LDD: Let me hasten to add this. Make sure you have the qualified people you need—lighting men, stage hands, sound men. If it hadn't been for Jerry's knowledge of all these things, we would have been lost. Another observation. The entertainment was excellent. The Communication was a memorable one. But the only lasting thing is our motion picture. That will go on for years, and as you have proven in other places, 25 to 50 years from now it can be the basis for an updated film.

AL: What about the mural?

LDD: That, too, is lasting, but it will be placed in one location. The film can go anywhere. Then we've got the time capsule. What a thrill those who open

Ethel Merman, the First Lady of the American Musical Theater, was the featured performer for the Gala Celebration in Williamsburg for the Grand Lodge of Virginia. Her musical director, Eric Knight, conducted the Richmond Symphony Orchestra, beginning with one of Knight's stirring compositions of an "American Medley." So well was Miss Merman's performance received by the thousands present, she, with Knight at the piano, gave a half hour encore. The Grand Master presented her an outstanding plaque; Eric Knight and Jacques Houtmann, director of the Richmond Symphony, were presented with specially engraved batons.

it a hundred years from now will receive. Just imagine how we would have felt to have been able to open one from a hundred years ago.

AL: One problem will be finding the equipment to play the recordings and film on?

WJH: We're considering putting equipment in it along with technical sheets telling them how to use them.

LDD: I'll bet there will be museums where this equipment will be available.

WJH: It wouldn't surprise me if there aren't companies to take care of things like this. It was only two years ago the country celebrated its Bicentennial. There were a lot of time capsules filled then. Just think of how valuable some of the things we put in today will be 100 years from now.

AL: Let's go back to entertainment for a moment, what should be considered when selecting this important feature?

WJH: You must look beyond yourself and consider the overall group to be entertained. You shouldn't select entertainment to appeal to a small group. Select something in the middle. We were fortunate to have selected one of the greatest living entertainers today—Ethel Merman, who along with her accompanist Eric Knight, will have those who were present talking for years.

"The Heritage and the Challenge" was painted by Ms. Fran Gayle to depict some of the historical highlights of Freemasonry in Virginia. In the center a Colonial Mason tells his young Brother the age-old story of Freemasonry. It is watched over by God, symbolized by the All-Seeing Eye overlooking the Temple of Solomon, from which much of the ritual of Masonry is derived. The homes of the Grand Lodge are shown, as are scenes of historical significance. The portraits are of Peyton Randolph, John Blair, James Mercer, George Washington, Edmund Randolph, John Marshall, John Dove, James Monroe, Dr. George Potts, and Alexander G. Babcock each of whom played important roles in Virginia Freemasonry. The mural was unveiled during the 200th Anniversary Communication in Williamsburg, February, 1978. Throughout the balance of the year it was displayed in each section of the Old Dominion. It is permanently displayed in the Grand Lodge office-museum where a tape recording tells its story.

AL: Did you receive the cooperation you needed, Doug?

LDD: For the most part, yes. The appendant bodies were tremendous. They worked with us throughout the year. And the one thing we must remember, in Freemasonry the Grand Master is the boss. Without the cooperation of John W. Lanningham in 1977 and Robert R. Kennedy, Jr., in 1978, we would not have accomplished what we did. They stood behind us all the way.

AL: I'm glad you mentioned that. Without the support of the Grand Master, little can be accomplished in Freemasonry. Wasn't one of them interviewed along with you on radio?

LDD: Through the intervention of Jerry we had two interviews on radio. Those helped give the listener a better perspective of Freemasonry and our Bicentennial. This was excellent public relations. Other Grand Lodges should do the same thing.

AL: There were many exhibits at Williamsburg, including the mural, and these were carried over the state. Who designed them?

LDD: Jerry and his Public Relations Committee. They had to be carpenters, artists, and just about everything. This is something a committee planning a celebration should take into consideration early. His committee did an outstanding job.

AL: As you went along, did you keep your plans flexible?

LDD: We did. And let me strongly suggest the need for a good public relations committee in conjunction with any event.

WJH: And always prepare for the unexpected. We had some trying moments when key people died, or were incapacitated. Always provide backup men.

AL: Too often the leadership doesn't know who can do what. Any suggestions about how to correct this?

WJH: More complete records should be kept on every member. His talents should be recorded and available. Then we can find the right man for the right job.

AL: How would you go about selecting the right man for the right job if you had the records you're speaking of?

WJH: By using those records. Because a man has a title doesn't mean he's right for the job. If I find I have a brain tumor, I'm not going to let a plumber operate because he has a Masonic title or is a friend of mine. I'm going to find the best surgeon I can. We should treat every assignment in Masonry, no matter what it is, in the same manner.

LDD: Jerry's now a Past Master, but he wasn't when he was chosen by the Grand Master to head the Public Relations Committee. What Jerry said is so true. Get the best man you can for the job. In Virginia we're fortunate to have a Jerry Harmon and an Allen Roberts.

208

AL: You've had a varied background, Jerry, how did you acquire it?

WJH: Through actual experience, the type you can't get any more. I've been technical director for shows, lighting and sound aspects as well, plus a performer, and worked as a booking agent and publicity agent. A book won't tell you all these things, you have to work at it.

AL: Are you saying experience is what you should look for in the men you want to help make an event a success?

WJH: That's what is needed, but you can't always find it, so you do the best you can.

AL: Without question, public relations is important. When you took over the committee, what did you do?

WJH: The committee had never been active and my knowledge of Masonry wasn't good. I had to determine what could and could not be done within the laws of Masonry. That's when I turned to you for the answers. I found that Masonry has as much leeway as any organization to use to a full extent all the tools of public relations. There is a resistance to the use of these tools, because many Masons are in the position I was, they don't really know what you can and can't do. And many of them have been in Masonry much longer than I have. The answer to this problem will ultimately lie in education. But Masonry can make exhibits, it can provide time capsules, it can have public entertainment programs if they are in good taste. But good common sense must dictate what is used and done. When I put my committee together, with the approval of the Grand Master, I kept the upcoming Bicentennial in mind. I tried to anticipate the things the Grand Lodge would want to do. So I picked the men accordingly. Then we got involved in many aspects unrelated to public relations. Some of these things were mentioned earlier.

AL: Did you select men who were active in their Lodges?

WJH: Most of them were not active; few of them were Past Masters, but they had the skills we needed. For instance, we found an inactive Mason who owned an exhibits business. Thank heavens he was willing to work with us. A building had been contracted for that had no props or anything else. Everything had to be improvised. We had to go outside of Masonry to find the proper people. I had to bring in three girls to handle the makeup. They contributed their talent. So did the soundman and the lighting operator. We made them feel a part of the entertainment production.

AL: There are some things, aren't there, where you must have Masons?

WJH: Oh, yes. The filming, for instance, had to be done by Masons. Even then things were filmed the general public shouldn't necessarily see, so Masons have to do the editing, too. And these cameramen should be informed about where and when something is to happen.

AL: We're getting back to communication again?

WJH: Communication is all-important. Without it you have a disaster.

LDD: And communication is important for an event to be a success as far as attendance is concerned. The members should be kept informed of what is planned, when and where.

AL: We can go on and on, but I think stopping on that one word—Communication—will leave our readers with something vital to think about. Thank you both for sharing your time and experience with us.

Several things stand out in this interview. For those planning any type of Lodge or Grand Lodge celebration, it will be well to read it again. There are several essential ingredients needed to be successful. The most important is GOOD COMMUNICATION. And try this for a formula:

Time + Talent + Money added to **Tender Loving Care = A Gala Celebration.**

Here's a good item with which to close this little book. It appeared in the Grand Secretary's Bulletin *of the Grand Lodge of Ohio, by my good friend Robert A. Hinshaw, Past Grand Master and Grand Secretary. It happened to cross my desk one day when I was despondent. It changed my outlook considerably. It just might do the same for you.*

When Things Go Wrong

When Things Go Wrong, as they sometimes will,
When the road you're trudging seems all up hill,
When the funds are low and the debts are high,
And you want to smile but you have to sigh,
When care is pressing you down a bit,
Rest, if you must, **But Don't You Quit.**

Life is queer with its twists and turns,
As every one of us sometimes learns,
And many a failure turns about
When he might have won had he stuck it out;
So don't give up, though the pace seems slow—
For you may succeed with another blow.

Often the goal is nearer than
It seems to a faint and faltering man,
Often the struggler has given up,
When he might have captured the victor's cup.
And he learned too late, when the night slipped down,
How close he was to the golden crown.

Success is failure, turned inside out—
The silver tint of the clouds of doubt—
And you never can tell how close you are,
It may be near when it seems afar;
So stick to the fight when you're hardest hit—
It's When Things Seem Worse That You Mustn't Quit!

—Author Unknown

INDEX

215

ABOUT THE AUTHOR

Allen E. Roberts was one of the first to earn the title of Certified Administrative Manager. He is the owner of Imagination Unlimited! and its subsidiary, Anchor Communications. For over forty years he has worked as a manager and leader. During World War II he earned the rank of Chief Commissary Steward in slightly over three years.

He has been an administrative assistant, administrative officer, office manager, business manager, and management consultant. His biography will be found in several of Marquis' *Who's Who* volumes. For almost forty years he has shared his managerial ability with the fraternity he loves—Freemasonry. A list of the books and motion pictures he has authored and produced are recorded in the front of this book. As this volume goes to press he is working on four more books and a motion picture.

Roberts is a Past Master of two Lodges: Babcock No. 322 and Virginia Research Lodge No. 1777. He has been Secretary of the latter for 15 years. He is a Past District Deputy Grand Master, a Past District Deputy Grand High Priest, a Past Deputy Grand Secretary, and is the Fraternal Reviewer and Chairman of the Fraternal Relations Committee of the Grand Chapter of Royal Arch Masons of Virginia.

He has been closely associated with the Masonic Service Association for more than 25 years, and has developed films and training aids, as well as Short Talk Bulletins for it.

His Honorary Memberships include: Babcock Lodge No. 322; American Union Lodge No. 1, Ohio; Vincennes Lodge No. 1, Indiana; Lodge St. Thomas No. 306, Scotland; Alexandria Lodge No. 33, New Brunswick, Canada; Research Lodge No. 106, Georgia; Masonic Lodge of Research of Connecticut; Tennessee Research Lodge; Richmond Chapter No. 3, RAM, Virginia; Josiah H. Drummond Council No. 1, Allied Masonic Degrees, Maine; and the Virginia Craftsmen, of which he is President *ad vitam*.

His citations include: Josiah Hayden Drummond Medal of Maine; Silver Medal of the General Grand Chapter, RAM; John Dove Distinguished Service Medal of the Grand Chapter, RAM, of Virginia; Medal of Excellence of the MLR of Connecticut; Glasgow Compass Association Gold Medal; Virginia Craftsmen Distinguished Service Medal; Red Branch of Erie of the

AMD. From the Order of DeMolay he has been awarded the Honorary Legion of Honor; the Cross of Honor; and White Honor Key.

He is a Fellow and Past President of the Philalethes Society and now its International Executive Secretary, and he holds its Certificate of Literature; a member of the Society of Blue Friars (Masonic authors); Secretary of the Masonic Brotherhood of the Blue Forget-Me-Not (Masonic educators and writers); Honorary citizen of several states; citations from several Grand Lodges and Masonic bodies; Honorary Fellow of the Phylaxis Society (Prince Hall Masons). He is a Past Grand Chancellor of the Grand Council of Rites; and is now the Grand Senior Deacon of the Grand Council, Allied Masonic Degrees.

He is a Methodist and speaks occasionally from pulpits. He has served in various civic capacities. He is married to Dorothy "Dottie" Grimes, and they have four sons and one daughter. They reside on sacred ground—where many of the Seven Days Battles were fought during the American Civil War.